Hot Cakes

Hot Cakes

Step-by-step recipes for 19 sensational, fun cakes

DEBBIE BROWN

METRO BOOKS
NEW YORK

Copyright © 2007 text and designs: Debbie Brown
Copyright © 2007 photographs: New Holland Publishers (UK) Ltd
Copyright © 2007 New Holland Publishers (UK) Ltd

ISBN-13: 978-1-4351-0185-2
ISBN-10: 1-4351-0185-5

Printed and bound in Malaysia

1 3 5 7 9 10 8 6 4 2

For Dave and Sue

Contents

Introduction

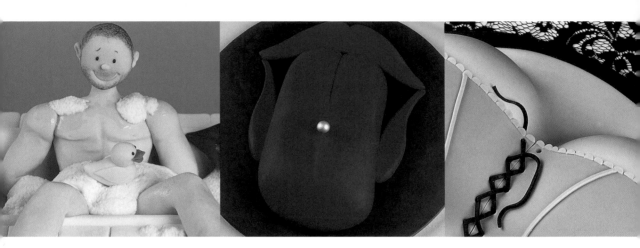

 Fun cakes with a naughty theme are always popular, mainly because of the peals of laughter that resound when the cake is presented. This sequel to Naughty Cakes contains some fun ideas, some slightly risqué but others along a funny and familiar theme. Images we see the world over like a builder bending down with the top of his bottom on show, (Builder's Bum, see page 54) and a fun bath scene with a nice hunky man getting ready for a night out (Scrub Up!, see page 20).

The designs can also be adapted to personalise a cake for the recipient by making some slight changes like hair colour, favourite

clothing, etc. It is a great compliment to see a caricature of
yourself in sugar and people are always impressed that you took
the time to make something special for them.

From beginners right through to experienced cake decorators,
this collection of naughty ideas will give you fun projects and
ideas that are achievable. Some projects are very quick and simple,
whilst others are a little more involved, giving you plenty of
choice on which xtra naughty cake you decide to make. No matter
which one you choose, your cake will be gratefully received and is
sure to be the fabulous centrepiece of any celebration.

Basic recipes

I would always recommend making your own cake base, as shop-bought versions do not produce the same results. Many specialist cake decorating suppliers will supply ready-made sugarpaste, modelling paste, royal icing and other ingredients, but you will find recipes for making your own in this section. All spoon measures are level unless otherwise stated.

MADEIRA SPONGE CAKE

I prefer to use a Madeira sponge cake recipe for all my cakes as you need a cake which is moist and light, but still suitable for carving and sculpting without crumbling. Shop-bought cake mixes and ready-made cakes will not produce the same results, as they are often too soft and crumbly to withstand sculpting into different shapes. For each of the cakes in this book, refer to the cake chart on page 11 for specific quantities and baking times, then follow the method given below.

1 Preheat the oven to 150–160°C/ 325°F/Gas mark 3, then grease and line your baking tin.
2 Sift the self-raising and plain (all-purpose) flours together in a bowl.
3 Soften the butter and place in a food mixer or large mixing bowl with the caster (superfine) sugar and beat until the mixture is pale and fluffy.
4 Add the eggs to the mixture one at a time with a spoonful of the flour, beating well after each addition. Add a few drops of vanilla extract.
5 Using a spatula or large spoon, fold the remaining flour into the mixture.
6 Spoon the mixture into the tin, then make a dip in the top of the mixture using the back of a spoon.
7 Bake in the centre of your oven for the time stated in the cake chart (see page 11), or until a skewer inserted in the centre comes out clean.

8 Leave to cool in the tin for five minutes, then turn out onto a wire rack and leave to cool completely. When cold, store in an airtight container or double wrap in clingfilm (plastic wrap) for at least eight hours, allowing the texture to settle before use.

MADEIRA CAKE VARIATIONS

CHOCOLATE MARBLE CAKE
Before spooning the cake mixture into the tin, fold in 200 g (7 oz) of melted chocolate until marbled. Fold in completely for a light chocolate cake.

CHOCOLATE ORANGE MARBLE CAKE
Follow the instructions for a Chocolate Marble Cake, adding the grated rind and juice of one organic orange.

LEMON CAKE
Add the grated rind and juice of one organic lemon to the cake mixture.

ORANGE AND LEMON CAKE
Add the grated rind of one organic orange and one lemon to the cake mixture and add a squeeze of orange juice.

COFFEE CAKE
Add two tablespoons of coffee essence to the cake mixture.

Madeira sponge cake

ALMOND
Add 1 teaspoon of almond essence and 2–3 tablespoons of ground almonds to the cake mixture.

BUTTERCREAM
Buttercream is very versatile as it is suitable as a cake filling as well as for creating a crumb coat. This seals the cake to stop it from drying out, and provides a good adhesive base for the sugarpaste coating. For intricately sculpted cakes, leave the buttercream crumb coat to set firmly, then add a little more or rework the surface to soften so that the sugarpaste will stick to the cake.

Makes 625 g / 1¼ lb / 3¾ c

- 175 g / 6 oz / ¾ c unsalted butter, softened
- 2–3 tbsp milk
- 1 tsp vanilla extract
- 450 g / 1 lb / 3¼ c icing (confectioners') sugar, sifted

1 Place the softened butter, milk and vanilla extract into a mixer. Add the icing sugar a little at a time, mixing on medium speed, until light, fluffy and pale in colour.
2 Store in an airtight container and use within 10 days. Bring to room temperature and beat again before use.

BUTTERCREAM VARIATIONS

CHOCOLATE
Add 90 g (3 oz) of good-quality melted chocolate, or use 3–4 tablespoons of cocoa powder mixed to a paste with milk.

ORANGE OR LEMON CURD
Add 2–3 tablespoons of orange or lemon curd.

COFFEE
Add 2–3 tablespoons of coffee essence.

RASPBERRY
Add 3–4 tablespoons of seedless raspberry jam.

ALMOND
Add 1 teaspoon almond essence.

SUGARPASTE
Good-quality ready-made sugarpaste is easy to use, produces good results and comes in a range of colours. It is readily available in large supermarkets and through specialist cake decorating outlets – see page 78

for a list of stockists and suppliers. However, if you prefer to make your own sugarpaste, try the following recipe. CMC is an abbreviation of Carboxymethyl Cellulose, an edible thickener widely used in the food industry. Check that it is food grade C1000P/E466. Gum tragacanth can be used as an alternative.

Makes 625 g / 1¼ lb / 3¾ c

- 1 egg white made up from dried egg albumen
- 2 tbsp liquid glucose
- 625 g / 1¼ lb / 3¾ c icing (confectioners') sugar
- A little white vegetable fat, if required
- A pinch of CMC or gum tragacanth, if required

1 Put the egg white and liquid glucose into a bowl, using a warm spoon for the liquid glucose.
2 Sift the icing sugar into the bowl, adding a little at a time and stirring until the mixture thickens.
3 Turn out onto a work surface dusted liberally with icing sugar and knead the paste until soft, smooth and pliable. If the paste is a little dry and cracked, fold in some vegetable fat and knead again. If the paste is soft and sticky, add a little more icing sugar or a pinch of CMC or gum tragacanth to stabilize.
4 Put immediately into a polythene bag and store in an airtight container. Keep at room temperature or refrigerate and use within a week. Bring back to room temperature and knead thoroughly before use. Home-made sugarpaste can be frozen for up to 3 months.

ROYAL ICING
Royal icing is used to pipe details such as hair, fur effect, etc. It is also used to stick items together, as when it dry it holds items firmly in place. Ready-made royal icing or powder form (follow instructions on the packet) can be obtained from supermarkets. To make your own, use this recipe.

Makes 75 g (2½ oz)
- 1 tsp egg albumen
- 1 tbsp water

Sugarpaste blocks

- 65–70 g / 2¼ oz / ½ c icing (confectioners') sugar

1 Put the egg albumen into a bowl. Add the water and stir until dissolved. Beat in the icing sugar a little at a time until the icing is firm, glossy and forms peaks if a spoon is pulled out.

2 To stop the icing from forming a crust, place a damp cloth over the top of the bowl until you are ready to use it, or transfer to an airtight container and refrigerate.

SUGAR GLUE

This recipe makes a strong sugar glue which works extremely well. Alternatively, ready-made sugar glue can be purchased from specialist cake decorating outlets.

- ¼ tsp CMC powder or gum tragacanth
- 2 tbsp water

1 Mix the CMC with water and leave to stand until the powder is fully absorbed. The glue should be smooth and have a soft dropping consistency.

2 If the glue thickens after a few days, add a few drops more water. Store in an airtight container in the refrigerator and use within one week.

3 To use, brush a thin coat over the surface of the item you wish to glue, leave for a few moments to become tacky, and then press in place.

MODELLING PASTE

Modelling paste is used for creating figures and other smaller modelled items as it is more flexible. This quick and easy recipe makes a high quality modelling paste, which has been used throughout the book.

- 450 g (1 lb) sugarpaste (see page 9)
- 1 tsp CMC powder or gum tragacanth

1 Knead the CMC into sugarpaste. The sugarpaste starts to thicken as soon as CMC is incorporated so it can be used immediately. More thickening will occur gradually over a period of 24 hours.

2 The amount of CMC can be varied depending on usage; a firmer paste is more suitable for limbs, miniature modelling etc., so a little more can be added. This tends to dry the paste much faster, so modelling should be done quickly. Simpler or larger modelled pieces should need less CMC. It is also dependent on room temperature, atmospheric conditions, etc., so adjust accordingly. Store in an airtight container and use within two weeks for best results.

QUICK PASTILLAGE

Pastillage is a fast-drying paste, suitable for creating tables (see page 68) as the paste dries extremely hard and will its keep shape.

Makes 260 g (9 oz) pastillage

- 2 tsp CMC powder or gum tragacanth
- 260 g (9 oz) royal icing

1 Mix the CMC or gum tragacanth into stiff-peaked royal icing. The mixture will thicken immediately. Knead on a work surface sprinkled liberally with icing sugar until the mixture forms a paste and is smooth and crack-free.

2 Keep in an airtight container and store in the refrigerator. Bring back to room temperature before use.

EDIBLE GLITTER

There is a lot of choice available through specialist cake decorating outlets for edible sparkling powders, but the glitters tend to be non-toxic food-safe, which I recommend be removed before serving. If you prefer to use something edible, try this quick and simple glitter recipe.

1 Mix equal parts (¼–½ tsp) gum arabic, water and your chosen edible metallic or sparkle powder food colouring. The mixture should look like thick paint.

2 Place a non-stick ovenproof liner/sheet onto a baking tray and brush the mixture over the surface. The mixture may congeal, so brush it out as thinly as possible. Bake on a very low heat for around ten minutes, until dry and starting to peel away from the liner.

3 Remove from oven and leave to cool. Lift with a palette knife and place into a sieve. Gently push through the sieve to produce small glitter particles. Store in a food-safe container.

SUGAR STICKS

These are used as edible supports, mainly to help hold modelled heads in place, but they can also be used for a variety of other purposes – flagpoles, for example – depending on their size.

Makes around 10–20 sugar sticks

- 1 level tsp stiff peak royal icing
- ¼ tsp CMC or gum tragacanth

1 Knead the CMC or gum tragacanth into the royal icing until the mixture forms a paste. Either roll it out and cut it into different sized strips of various lengths using a plain-bladed knife, or roll individual thin paste sausages. Let dry on a sheet of foam, preferably overnight. When dry, store in an airtight container.

Cake chart

To create the cakes in this book you will need to refer to this cake chart for specific quantities and baking times, then simply follow the appropriate method given on page 8.

- **SAUCY STOCKINGS**
- **SEXY BASQUE**

2 x 1 litre (2 pint) ovenproof bowls or 16 cm (6½ in) spherical tin

Unsalted butter, softened . . 285 g/10 oz/1¼ c
Caster (superfine) sugar . . . 285 g/10 oz/1½ c
Large eggs 5
Self-raising flour . . . . 285 g /10 oz/2½ c
Plain (all-purpose flour) . . . 145 g/5 oz/1¼ c
Baking time . . . . 1¼–1½ hours

- **SHOWGIRLS**

2 x 15 cm (6 in) round tins

Unsalted butter, softened . . 285 g/10 oz/1¼ c
Caster (superfine) sugar . . . 285 g/10 oz/1½ c
Large eggs 5
Self-raising flour . . . . 285 g/10 oz/2½ c
Plain (all-purpose flour) . . . 145 g/5 oz/1¼ c
Baking time . . . . 1¼–1½ hours

- **SEXY HEELS**
- **HOT BOXERS**

25 cm (10 in) square shaped tin

Unsalted butter, softened . . 340 g/12 oz/1½ c
Caster (superfine) sugar . . . 340 g/12 oz/1¾ c
Large eggs 6
Self-raising flour . . . . 340 g/12 oz/3 c
Plain (all-purpose flour) . . . 175 g/6 oz/1½ c
Baking time . . . . 50 minutes–1¼ hour

- **BUILDER'S BUM**

25 cm (10 in) round tin

Unsalted butter, softened . . 400 g/14 oz/1⅔ c
Caster (superfine) sugar . . . 400 g/14 oz/2 c
Large eggs 7
Self-raising flour . . . . 400 g/14 oz/3½ c
Plain (all-purpose flour) . . . 200 g/7 oz/1⅔ c
Baking time . . . . 1½–1¾ hours

- **CENTERFOLD**

30 x 25 cm (12 x 10 in) oblong tin

Unsalted butter, softened . . 400 g/14 oz/1⅔ c
Caster (superfine) sugar . . . 400 g/14 oz/2 c
Large eggs 7
Self-raising flour . . . . 400 g/14 oz/3½ c
Plain (all-purpose flour) . . . 200 g/7 oz/1⅔ c
Baking time . . . . 1¼–1½ hours

- **HOT DEVIL**

20 cm (8 in) and 15 cm (6 in) round tins

Unsalted butter, softened . . 340 g/12 oz/1½ c
Caster (superfine) sugar . . . 340 g/12 oz/1¾ c
Large eggs 6
Self-raising flour . . . . 340 g/12 oz/3 c
Plain (all-purpose flour) . . . 175 g/6 oz/1½ c
Baking time . . . . 1–1¼ hours

- **BIRTHDAY TREAT**
- **SCRUB UP!**

25 cm (10 in) square tin

Unsalted butter, softened . . 400 g/14 oz/1⅔ c
Caster (superfine) sugar . . . 400 g/14 oz/2 c
Large eggs 7
Self-raising flour . . . . 400 g/14 oz/3½ c
Plain (all-purpose flour) . . . 200 g/7 oz/1⅔ c
Baking time . . . . 1½–1¾ hours

- **PIERCED TONGUE**

30 cm (12 in) square tin

Unsalted butter, softened . . 340 g/12 oz/1½ c
Caster (superfine) sugar . . . 340 g/12 oz/1¾ c
Large eggs 6
Self-raising flour . . . . 340 g/12 oz/3 c
Plain (all-purpose flour) . . . 175 g/6 oz/1½ c
Baking time . . . . 50 minutes–1¼ hour

- **SEXY SANTA**

2 x 15 cm (6 in) square tins

Unsalted butter, softened . . 285 g/10 oz/1¼ c
Caster (superfine) sugar . . . 285 g/10 oz/1½ c
Large eggs 5
Self-raising flour . . . . 285 g/10 oz/2½ c
Plain (all-purpose flour) . . . 145 g/5 oz/1¼ c
Baking time . . . . 50 minutes–1 hour

- **CAMPING FUN**
- **LAST NIGHT OF FREEDOM**

23 cm (9 in) and 20 cm (8 in) round tins

Unsalted butter, softened . . 400 g/14 oz/1⅔ c
Caster (superfine) sugar . . . 400 g/14 oz/2 c
Large eggs 7
Self-raising flour . . . . 400 g/14 oz/3½ c
Plain (all-purpose flour) . . . 200 g/7 oz/1⅔ c
Baking time . . . . 1½–1¾ hours

- **21-BUM SALUTE**

20 cm (8 in), 15 cm (6 in) and 10 cm (4 in) round tins

Unsalted butter, softened . . 400 g/14 oz/1⅔ c
Caster (superfine) sugar . . . 400 g/14 oz/2 c
Large eggs 7
Self-raising flour . . . . 400 g/14 oz/3½ c
Plain (all-purpose flour) . . . 200 g/7 oz/1⅔ c
Baking time . . . . 50 minutes–1½ hours

- **PIN-UP GIRL**
- **PANTIES!**

20 cm (8 in) round tin

Unsalted butter, softened . . 285 g/10 oz/1¼ c
Caster (superfine) sugar . . . 285 g/10 oz/1½ c
Large eggs 5
Self-raising flour . . . . 285 g/10 oz/2½ c
Plain (all-purpose flour) . . . 145 g/5 oz/1¼ c
Baking time . . . . 1–1¼ hours

- **WILD WEST DANCERS**

6 x 10 cm (4 in) round tins

Unsalted butter, softened . . 285 g/10 oz/1¼ c
Caster (superfine) sugar . . . 285 g/10 oz/1½ c
Large eggs 5
Self-raising flour . . . . 285 g/10 oz/2½ c
Plain (all-purpose flour) . . . 145 g/5 oz/1¼ c
Baking time . . . . 50 minutes–1 hour

- **CUPCAKE UNDIES**

12 hole bun tin

Unsalted butter, softened . . 115 g/5 oz/½ c
Caster (superfine) sugar . . . 115 g/5 oz/⅔ c
Large eggs 2
Self-raising flour . . . . 115 g/5 oz/¾ c
Plain (all-purpose flour) . . . 60 g/2 oz/½ c
Baking time . . . . 30 minutes

Basic techniques

Cake decorating is easier than it looks, although it can seem a little daunting if you are a complete beginner. This section shows you a few simple, basic techniques that will help you achieve great results and professional-looking cakes.

SCULPTING A CAKE

The first rule of cake sculpting is to have a moist but firm sponge cake that will not crumble. I recommend that you follow the recipes and method given in this book for a Madeira sponge cake (see page 8). If you are tempted to buy a cake mix or a ready-baked cake, make sure that it won't crumble away as soon as you start to cut into it. Ready-made cakes are really only suitable for projects involving minimal sculpting and stacking of layers.

Use a serrated knife for cake carving. When trimming away the crust of a cake, keep the cake as level as possible so there are no problems with balance if the cake is being stacked. Use a ruler for straight cuts and be aware of the knife blade, keeping it in the correct position for the cut you need.

ROLLING OUT SUGARPASTE

Sugarpaste can be rolled out successfully on any even food-safe

Rolling out sugarpaste

work surface, but I recommend that you use a large polypropylene board and rolling pin, both of which have tough, smooth surfaces.

Start by dusting your worksurface lightly with icing (confectioners') sugar. Knead the sugarpaste thoroughly, until soft and warm. Sugarpaste can start to dry out when exposed to the air, so roll out as quickly and evenly as possible to a covering thickness of around 3–4 mm (⅛ in), moving the paste around after each roll using a sprinkling of icing (confectioners') sugar. Make sure there isn't a build up of sugarpaste or icing (confectioners') sugar on either your board or your rolling pin, to help keep the sugarpaste perfectly smooth. Sugarpaste can stick to the work surface very quickly. If this happens, re-knead and start again.

COLOURING SUGARPASTE

Some brands of ready-made sugarpaste are available in a range of

Sculpting a cake

Colouring sugarpaste

Covering a cake board with sugarpaste

Covering a cake with sugarpaste

colours but I usually prefer to mix my own colours. The best food colourings are obtainable as a paste or concentrated liquid. Avoid the watery liquid food colourings and powder colours, unless you want to achieve very pale shades. Powder food colours are usually only used to brush over the surface of dried sugarpaste to enhance certain areas.

The best way to apply food colour paste is with the tip of a knife. Simply dab a block of sugarpaste with the end of a knife (if you are creating a new colour, remember to keep a record of how many "dabs" of paste you use). Add a little at a time until the required shade is achieved. Knead thoroughly after each addition until the colour is even. Bear in mind that the colour will deepen slightly on standing, so be careful not to add too much.

If you wish to colour a large amount of sugarpaste, colour a small ball first, and then knead into the remaining amount to disperse the colour quickly. Wearing plastic gloves or rubbing a little white vegetable fat over your hands can help when colouring deep shades, as this can prevent a lot of mess. Some food colours can temporarily stain your hands.

COVERING A CAKE BOARD WITH SUGARPASTE

Knead the sugarpaste thoroughly until soft and warm. Roll out to roughly the size and shape of the cake board,

using a sprinkling of icing (confectioners') sugar and move around after each roll to prevent sticking.

Place the rolling pin on the centre of the rolled out sugarpaste and lift the back half over the top. Hold both ends of the rolling pin, lift and position the sugarpaste against the cake board and unroll over the top. Roll the rolling pin gently over the surface to stick the sugarpaste firmly to the board. If the sugarpaste is still loose, moisten along the outside edge only, using a little water or sugar glue on a brush.

Rub the surface with a cake smoother for a smooth, dimple-free surface. Lift the cake board and trim away the excess around the outside edge using a plain-bladed knife. Keep the knife straight to gain a neat edge, carefully removing any residue along the blade for a clean cut.

COVERING A CAKE WITH SUGARPASTE

Before applying sugarpaste to the buttercream-covered surface of a cake, make sure the buttercream is soft and sticky by reworking a little using a knife, or by adding a little more. Roll the sugarpaste out approximately 15 cm (6 in) larger than the top of the cake to allow enough icing to cover the sides of the cake. You can lift and position the sugarpaste on the cake as you would to cover a cake board, and then press the sugarpaste gently but firmly in position, smoothing over the

surface using your hands. Rub gently with your hands over any small cracks to blend them in. If you have any gaps, stroke the sugarpaste surface to stretch it slightly. Trim away excess any using a plain-bladed knife.

OBTAINING A GOOD FINISH

You will invariably find that you have occasional bumps on the surface of your cake or trapped air bubbles. A cake smoother is invaluable for obtaining a perfectly smooth finish for your sugarpaste. Rub firmly but gently in a circular motion to remove any small dents or bumps.

Any excess icing (confectioners') sugar can be brushed off dried sugarpaste. With stubborn areas, use a slightly damp large soft bristle pastry brush. The moisture will melt the excess, but take care not to wet the surface as streaks may result.

Obtaining a good finish

General equipment

There is a huge selection of cake decorating tools and equipment available now. Listed below are the basic necessities for cake decorating, some of which you likely already have in your kitchen. I've also added some specialist items that can help achieve great results.

1. WORKBOARD
You can easily work on any washable, even work surface, but for best results use a non-stick polypropylene work board. They are available in various sizes, with non-slip feet on the reverse.

2. ROLLING PINS
Polypropylene rolling pins are available in a variety of lengths, but basic large and small pins are the most useful.

3. SERRATED KNIFE
A medium-sized serrated knife is invaluable when sculpting a cake, as it cuts away neatly when using a slight sawing action.

4. PLAIN-BLADED KNIFE
Small and medium plain-bladed knives are used to cut through paste cleanly and evenly.

5. PALETTE KNIFE
This is used for the smooth spreading of buttercream, and also to help lift modelled pieces easily from a work surface.

6. CAKE SMOOTHER
Smoothes the surface of sugarpaste to remove any bumps or indents by rubbing gently in a circular motion.

7. SUGAR SHAKER
A handy container filled with icing (confectioners') sugar. Used for sprinkling the work surface before rolling out paste.

8. PAINTBRUSHES
Available in various sizes, choose good quality sable paintbrushes for painting details. Use a flat-ended brush for dusting powder food colours over the surface of dried paste.

9. LARGE PASTRY BRUSH
Invaluable for brushing excess icing (confectioners') sugar and crumbs away. When dampened slightly, it will lift any stubborn residue icing (confectioners') sugar from the surface quickly and easily.

10. RULER
Used for approximate measuring during cake and paste cutting and for indenting neat lines in sugarpaste.

11. SCISSORS
Needed for general use of cutting templates, piping bags and some small detailing.

12. PLAIN PIPING TUBES
Not only are these tubes used for piping royal icing, they are also used as cutters and indenters. For finer cuts use good quality metal tubes in preference to plastic ones.

13. PAPER PIPING BAGS
For use with royal icing. Parchment or greaseproof paper piping bags are available ready-made from cake decorating suppliers.

14. COCKTAIL STICKS
Readily available in food-safe wood or plastic form, these are useful for marking any fine detailing in paste.

15. FOAM PIECES
Used to support modelled pieces whilst drying, as the air can circulate all around. When the piece is dry, the foam is easily squeezed smaller for easy removal.

16. CUTTERS
Available in an array of different styles and shapes. Metal cutters usually have finer, cleaner edges but are more expensive. Some small cutters have plungers to remove the cut out shape.

17. TURNTABLE
When working on a cake, placing on a turntable allows you to quickly and easily move the cake around. Some bakers find it invaluable as it lifts the cake to a higher level.

18. FOOD COLOURING
Paste colours are suitable for colouring paste and royal icing, while powder colours add a subtle hue when brushed onto the surface of dried sugarpaste.

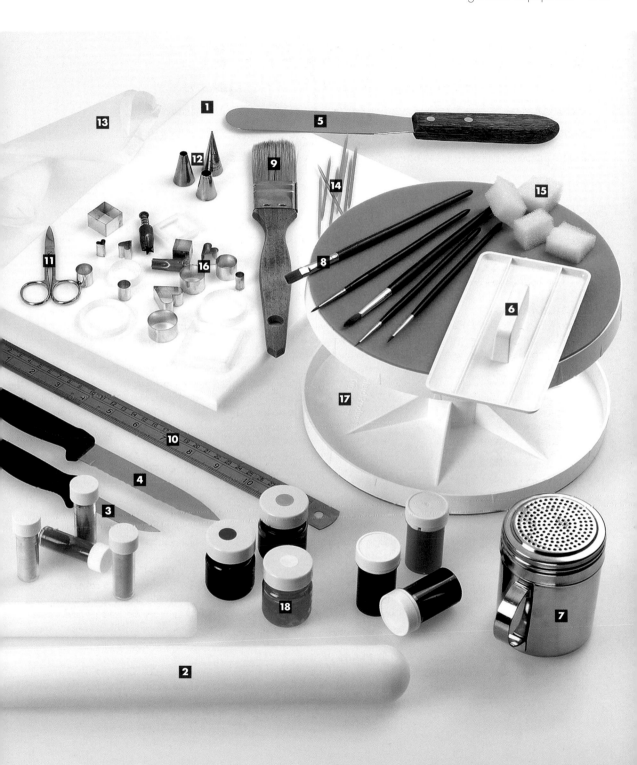

Showgirls

Three glamorous showgirls scantily dressed in glitz and glitter dancing out of a stylish top hat will be a sure winner for any special male celebration.

YOU WILL NEED

- 2 x 15 cm (6 in) round sponge cakes (see page 11)
- 25-cm (10-in) round cake board
- 20-cm (8-in) cake card
- 550 g / 1 lb 3½ oz / 2¾ c buttercream (see page 8)
- Icing (confectioners') sugar in a sugar shaker
- Sugar glue and paintbrush
- 3 x sugar sticks (see page 10)
- Red and black food colouring paste
- Edible silver powder
- Edible or food-safe royal blue and silver glitter
- A few drops of clear alcohol (e.g. vodka, gin)

SUGARPASTE (see page 9)

- 340 g (12 oz) white
- 1.15 kg (2 lb 8½ oz) dark grey

MODELLING PASTE (see page 10)

- 260 g (9 oz) black
- 200 g (7 oz) flesh-colour
- 30 g (1 oz) royal blue
- 20 g (¾ oz) white

EQUIPMENT

- Plain-bladed kitchen knife
- Serrated carving knife
- Large and small rolling pins
- Ruler
- Cake smoother
- Palette knife
- A few cocktail sticks
- Small pieces of foam (for support)
- 3 x 30-cm (12-in) food-safe dowelling
- Small blossom plunger cutter
- Various star cutters
- Medium and fine paintbrushes

1 Slightly dampen the cake board with water. Roll out the white sugarpaste using a sprinkling of icing sugar and cover the cake board, trimming excess from around the edge. Set aside to dry.

2 Trim the crust from each cake and level the tops. Cut a layer in each cake and stack one on top of each other. Shape the sides of the cake to slope inwards centrally, and then sandwich all layers together with buttercream. Spread buttercream on the underside of the cake, place centrally on the cake board and then spread a thin layer over the surface of the cake as a crumb coat and to help the paste stick.

TIP: If short of time, this cake will look just as spectacular with just one showgirl. Make her slightly larger and add more stars instead of plumes and feathers to her headdress.

Covering with sugarpaste

3 Roll out 120 g (4¼ oz) of dark grey sugarpaste and cover the top of the cake trimming around the top edge neatly. Roll out 625 g (1¼ lb) and cut a strip measuring the depth of the cake and 45 cm (18 in) in length. Dust with icing (confectioners') sugar and gently roll up. Place the open end against the side of the cake and unroll around the sides trimming excess at join **(see above)**. Using a little sugar glue, smooth the join closed.

4 For the hatband, thinly roll out 115 g (4 oz) of black modelling paste and cut a strip measuring at least 45 cm (18 in) in length and 4 cm (1½ in) deep. Roll up as before and stick around the top edge of the cake using a little sugar glue to secure.

5 To make the hat rim, first cut out a 13-cm (5-in) circle from the centre of the cake card, making a card ring. Thickly roll out the remaining dark grey sugarpaste, pushing a hole in the centre to spread out wider. Dampen the card slightly with a little water and cover the card ring. Smooth the inside and outside edges to round off, trimming excess away. Using a little glue, stick the rim centrally on top of the cake.

6 To make the canes, first roll 30 g (1 oz) of black modelling paste into a sausage and press flat. Moisten down the centre with sugar glue and then press a dowelling firmly into the centre. Pinch up the sides, closing the join and covering the dowelling 2.5 cm (1 in) from the top and 16 cm (6½ in) in length, leaving one third uncovered at the bottom. This uncovered part will be inserted into the cake. To gain a smooth surface, roll gently backwards and forwards over the work surface trimming excess straight at either end. Cover two more dowelling in the same way. Gently push each down into the cake with the central cane positioned slightly forward and the two either side angled outwards.

7 Split 10 g (¼ oz) of black modelling paste into three equally sized pieces. To make the top of each cane, shape into teardrop shapes and press both ends to flatten on the work surface. Moisten the top of each cane and then press these pieces onto the top with the fuller part uppermost, moulding around the dowelling until level with the black covering and trim any excess away.

8 To make a girl's body, shape 50 g (1¾ oz) of flesh-colour into a fat sausage. One-third from the top, roll gently backwards and forwards to narrow the waist, rounding off both ends. Roll the smaller end further to lengthen for the top of the body. Pinch up the neck, stroking gently to smooth.

Making the body

Lay the body down to flatten the front, pressing gently. Slice the neck and bottom straight. Indent a line for the bottom using a cocktail stick and then stand the body up making sure the figure is completely balanced. Indent the belly button using the cocktail stick. Make a hole in the neck using the cocktail stick, remove and then push in a sugar stick leaving a little protruding at the top. Make two further bodies and set each aside (**see below left**).

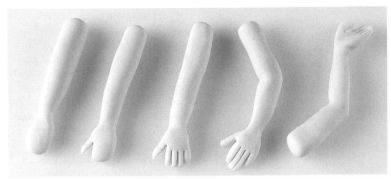

Making the arms

9 To make a head, roll 10 g (¼ oz) of flesh-colour into an oval shape and press down on the work surface to slightly flatten the face. Stroke around the chin area to sharpen the edge and indent either side to narrow, making a neat gently shaped chin. Push a cocktail stick into the base, making a hole for the sugar stick support, remove, and then stick the head onto the body using a little sugar glue to secure. Make two more heads as before.

10 Split 20 g (¾ oz) of flesh-coloured modelling paste into six equally sized pieces and use to make the arms. To make an arm, roll into a sausage shape and pinch gently at one end to round off for a hand. Press either side of the hand to lengthen into an oval shape and press onto the top to flatten slightly, without indenting. Make a cut no further than halfway down on one side for the thumb. Make three slightly shorter cuts along the top to separate fingers and smooth gently to lengthen, then press together and bend round. To naturally shape the hand, push the thumb towards the palm from the wrist. Lay the arm down and push in halfway, bend gently and then pinch out at the back to shape the elbow (**see above**). Stick onto the body in an upright position with the hands turned outwards, supported with a piece of

foam until dry. Make five further arms, cutting left and right hands, and attach to the bodies.

11 Using the remaining flesh-colour, roll into ball shapes for the boobs. Make three noses and stick in place on the face just below halfway. Model six oval shaped eyes using black modelling paste trimmings.

12 To make the headscarves, split 15 g (½ oz) of royal blue modelling paste into three equally sized pieces and shape into flattened circles. Wrap the circles around the back of each head, leaving the top open slightly for the plumes and feathers to be inserted later. Roll out a pea sized amount of royal blue and cut out six flowers using the blossom plunger cutter, sticking each in place using a little sugar glue. Roll out another pea-sized amount and cut three thin triangles for the front of each thong. Stick in place and then using a cocktail stick, indent little holes for the thong straps.

13 Using the white modelling paste, roll into different sized long teardrop shaped plumes and arrange on the top of each head, sticking together to secure. To make

the feather boas, split 5 g (just under ¼ oz) of white into three pieces and roll into long sausages. Press each flat and then make angled cuts along each side to feather the edges. For the royal blue feathers, roll different sized long thin teardrop shapes and cut as before (**see below**). Stick in place supported against the plumes.

14 Roll out the remaining black modelling paste and cut out all the stars. Dilute the edible silver powder with a few drops of clear alcohol and paint the stars using the medium paintbrush. Whilst each is still tacky, sprinkle with edible silver glitter. Stick in place when dry. Paint the cane tops silver and highlight along the thong straps. Paint the red lips, ultra fine black eyelashes and eyebrows using the fine paintbrush. Brush a little sugar glue onto the top of each hat and sprinkle royal blue glitter over the top.

Making the plumes

Scrub Up!

A good soak is probably a regular weekend occurrence for most single men getting ready to hit the town. Is he your dream date? It looks like he's only got the duck for company tonight...

YOU WILL NEED

- 25 cm (10 in) square sponge cake (see page 11)
- 30 cm (12 in) square cake board
- 550 g / 1 lb 3½ oz / 2¾ c buttercream (see page 8)
- Icing (confectioners') sugar in a sugar shaker
- Sugar glue and paintbrush
- 1 x sugar stick (see page 10)
- Black food colouring paste
- Clear piping gel

SUGARPASTE (see page 9)

- 1.5 kg (3 lb 5 oz) white

MODELLING PASTE (see page 10)

- 45 g (1½ oz) black
- 270 g (9½ oz) flesh
- 5 g (just under ¼ oz) pale grey
- Tiny ball of blue
- 30 g (1 oz) red
- 5 g (just under ¼ oz) yellow

EQUIPMENT

- Plain-bladed kitchen knife
- Ruler
- 1 cm (½ in) and 2.5 cm (1 in) square cutters
- Serrated carving knife
- Large and small rolling pins
- Cake smoother
- Palette knife
- A few cocktail sticks
- Small pieces of foam (for support)
- New pan scourer
- 1 cm (½ in) and 0.5 cm (¼ in) circle cutters
- Miniature heart cutter
- Fine and medium paintbrushes

1 Slightly dampen the cake board with water. Roll out 450 g (1 lb) of white sugarpaste using a sprinkling of icing sugar and cover the cake board, trimming excess from around the edge. Using a ruler, measure and indent lines 5 cm (2 in) apart to mark a tiled effect.

2 Cut out a line of small squares for the inset tiles at the front and back using the 1 cm (½ in) square cutter. Knead a little white sugarpaste and black modelling paste together until streaky and roll out and cut out black marbled inset tiles and slot in place. Set the cake board aside to dry.

3 Trim the crust from the cake and cut the cake in half using the ruler to measure exactly. Cut a layer in each half and sandwich three layers one on top of each other. Spread the underside with buttercream and position on the cake board leaving just over 10 cm (4 in) space at the front.

TIP: A fun idea would be to model some extra feet and arrange them in the bath 'water'. They're sure to be noticed quickly!

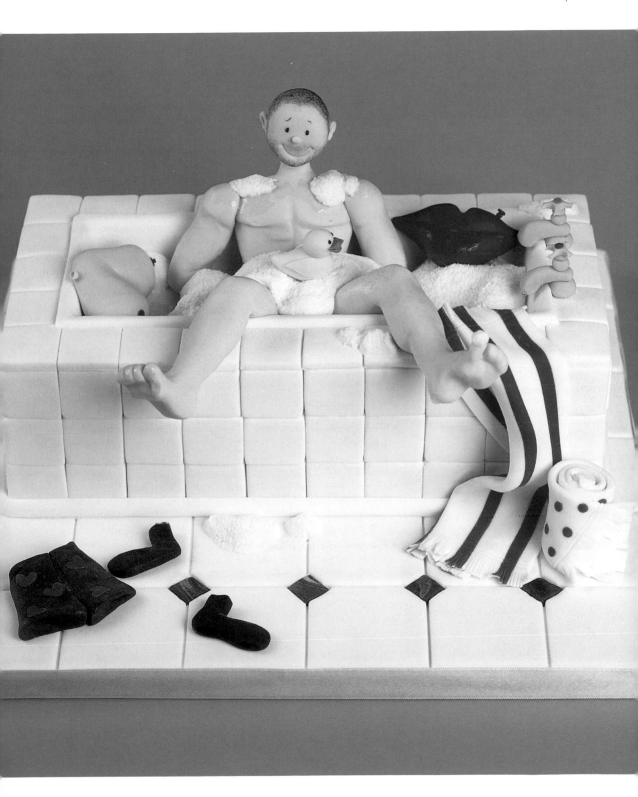

4 Place the fourth layer on top and cut out the inside leaving a 2.5 cm (1 in) edge and remove **(see below)**. Sandwich this edging in place with buttercream. The cake should measure exactly 8 cm (3 in) in height for the 2.5 cm (1 in) square tiles to fit properly. Spread a layer of buttercream over the surface of the cake as a crumb coat and help the sugarpaste stick.

Shaping cake

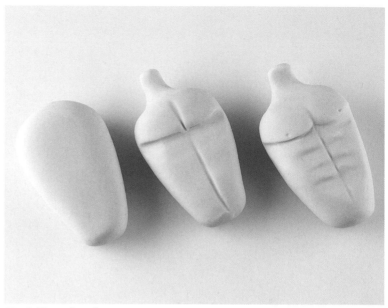

Modelling the chest

5 Using 650 g (1 lb 7 oz) of white, roll out and cut squares for tiles using the 2.5 cm (1 in) square cutter. Build up the tiles from the bottom of the cake, covering the two ends of the bath first (these tiles may need adjusting slightly as the area may be smaller after removing cake crust), then cover the back and front of the cake. When a side is covered, press the tiles in place firmly with a cake smoother.

6 Stick a layer of tiles around the top edge of the bath. Roll out 175 g (6 oz) of white and cover the inside of the bath, smoothing around the shape and along the outside edge and then trim excess to neaten.

7 The body is made up in pieces and arranged in the bath. Make the chest area first by shaping a rounded teardrop with 75 g (2½ oz) of flesh modelling paste and press to flatten slightly. Pinch up a neck at the full end. Mark a line down the centre. Roll the paintbrush handle from the bottom up to gain excess for the pectorals, smooth- ing a curve on the underside of each and indenting with a cocktail stick.

8 Mark three lines across the stomach. Rub gently over the surface to soften the markings **(see above)** and then stick in position in the bath. Push the sugar stick down through the neck, leaving a little protruding to hold his head in place.

9 For the arms, split 45 g (1½ oz) of flesh modelling paste in half. To make an arm, roll into a sausage shape and gently pinch one end to round off a hand and narrow the wrist. Push in halfway, pinching out at the back to shape the elbow. Indent at the top for a large muscle. Make the second arm.

10 Make the legs using 90 g (3 oz) of flesh modelling paste split into two. To make a leg, roll one half into a sausage and bend one end for the foot, pinching up gently to shape the heel. Pinch around the ankle. Cut toes, pinching up the large toe and stroke down the other toes so they curve underneath. Lay the leg down and push in at the back halfway between the ankle and the top of the leg, pinching the front to shape the knee **(see above right)**. Make the second leg and stick in position in the bath supported by foam pieces.

11 Model an oval-shaped head, nose and ears using 15 g (¾ oz) of flesh modelling paste, marking his wide grin by indenting the 1 cm (½ in) circle cutter in at an angle and a cocktail stick to dimple the corners. Stick in place over the sugar stick making sure the head is well balanced and then secure with a little sugar glue. Add two tiny black oval-shaped eyes.

15 To make the lips bath pillow, roll 20 g (¾ oz) of red into a tapering sausage and press flat. Mark a line in the centre using a knife and indent the top lip. Turn up the corners so the lips smile. Make the blower as before.

16 For the duck, model a teardrop shaped body and stick on a ball shaped head. For wings, shape two small teardrop shapes and press flat, sticking in place either side of the body. To make the beak, knead a tiny amount of yellow and red together making orange. Model an oval shape, press flat and fold in half. Stick in place pressing the top beak upwards slightly. Add two tiny black eyes.

17 With the remaining black, model two socks and the pair of boxer shorts, marking the waistband and fly with a knife. Thinly roll out the remaining red and cut out hearts to decorate the boxers.

18 Pour a little clear piping gel into the bath and using a cocktail stick, add little drips around the cake, on the taps and the man's big toe. Wipe a little piping gel over the man's shoulders, legs and over the lips bath pillow. Dilute a little black food colouring paste with a few drops of water and paint the fine eyebrows. Using the medium paintbrush with only a tiny amount of diluted black, stipple the hair, beard and moustache, building up the colour little by little. Any painted mistakes can be lifted off with a clean damp brush.

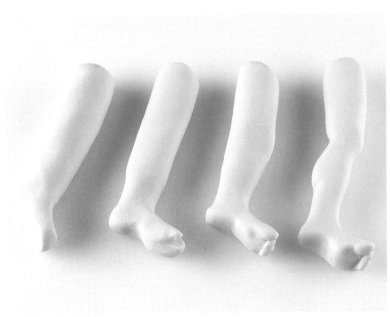

Making the legs

12 For the boob bath pillow, shape the remaining flesh into a large teardrop shape and roll the knife up from the full end to separate the boobs. Add a tiny ball and a little circle for the blower, indenting into the circle with the end of a paintbrush. For the nipples, add two tiny circles and dots of red modelling paste.

13 Press 145 g (5 oz) of white into the bath and texture using a pan scourer to give a bubble effect. Add small textured pieces around the bath, on his shoulders and a small piece on his big toe. For towels, thinly roll out the remaining white sugarpaste and cut out oblong shapes, decorating each with thinly rolled out and cut red strips and circles. Cut a frilled edge at the end of each. Fold over the dotty towel and drape the striped towel over the edge of the bath.

Forming the taps

14 Using the step picture as a guide, make the taps using grey modelling paste. The top of the tap is a flattened circle with four circles cut around the edge using the small circle cutter. Add a little red and blue circle on the top of each **(see above)**.

21-Bum Salute

This cheeky salute with a mix of fun and risqué dressed bums is perfect for a 21st birthday celebration for either a boy or a girl.

YOU WILL NEED

- 20 cm (8 in), 15 cm (6 in) and 10 cm (4 in) round sponge cakes (see page 11)
- 30 cm (12 in) round cake board
- 15 cm (6 in) and 10 cm (4 in) round cake cards
- 600 g / 1 lb 5¼ oz / 2½ c buttercream (see page 8)
- Icing (confectioners') sugar in a sugar shaker
- Sugar glue and paintbrush

SUGARPASTE (see page 9)

- 1.8 kg (4 lb) white

MODELLING PASTE (see page 10)

- 210 g (7½ oz) pale brown
- 650 g (1 lb 7 oz) pale flesh
- 660 g (1 lb 7¼ oz) flesh
- 90 g (3 oz) white
- 75 g (2½ oz) red
- 75 g (2½ oz) pale green

EQUIPMENT

- Plain-bladed kitchen knife
- Serrated carving knife
- Large and small rolling pins
- Cake smoother
- Palette knife
- Assorted thin ribbon trim
- A few cocktail sticks
- Small pieces of foam (for support)
- No.3 and 18 plain piping tubes (to cut circles)
- Miniature heart cutter

Covering the cakes

1 Slightly dampen the cake board with water. Roll out 400 g (14 oz) of white sugarpaste using a sprinkling of icing sugar and cover the cake board, trimming excess from around the edge. Set aside to dry.

2 Trim the crust from each cake and level the tops. Cut a layer in each cake and sandwich together with buttercream. Spread buttercream on the underside of each cake, place the largest cake centrally on the cake board and then place the other two cakes on a cake card. Spread a thin layer over the surface of each cake as a crumb coat and to help the paste stick.

3 Using the remaining white sugarpaste, roll out and cover the cakes completely, covering the largest cake first, smoothing down and around the shape and trimming excess from around the edge (**see left**). Smooth with a cake smoother and then stack centrally one on top of each other. Attach the ribbon trim around the base of each cake securing with a little sugar glue. You may need to insert the end of the ribbon into the sugarpaste covering slightly to help hold it in place. This can then be covered by one of the 'bums'.

4 Make three bums in pale brown and nine each in pale flesh and flesh. To make a bum, roll 75 g (2½ oz) of modelling paste into an oval shape and mark a line by indenting with the back of a knife **(see below)**. Cut the front straight, and stick in place against the cake. The top bum is left rounded.

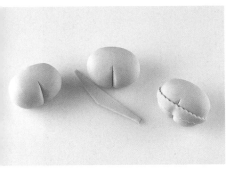

Assembling the bums

5 Using thinly rolled out white, red and pale green modelling paste, make all the underwear and decoration. The boxers are made from oblong strips of paste. The panties are made from triangular pieces of paste. Make some underwear and decorate the boxers and panties with stripes, circles and hearts. Use the cutters and different sized circles from the piping tubes, also using the wide end.

6 For frilled edging on panties, indent along the edge of the modelling paste with the end of a paintbrush. For the tartan effect on the boxers, position different width strips in a tartan pattern then gently roll over the surface to inlay. For the textured panties, press the large piping tube repeatedly over the surface. Use a cocktail stick to indent a dotty pattern.

The rear view of the cake

7 Using 10g (¼ oz) of white modelling paste, roll sausages and bend into the numerals. Lay flat until dry. For the arm, roll a sausage of flesh tapering it slightly and bend two thirds along the length for the elbow, pinching out at the back. Stick the shoulder in place against the base of the no.1 numeral.

8 Use 5 g (just under ¼ oz) of white for the glove. Stick a small ball onto the end of the arm and then push the end of the paintbrush into it to make a hole for the hand to slot in.

To make the hand, roll a teardrop shape and press onto the top to flatten slightly, without indenting. Make a cut no further than halfway down on one side for the thumb. Make three slightly shorter cuts along the top to separate fingers and smooth gently to lengthen, then press together and bend round. To naturally shape the hand, push the thumb towards the palm from the wrist. Stick in place in a salute and when completely dry, stick in place on top of the cake.

Sexy Heels

Who could resist this gorgeous pair of stilettos with matching shoebox? Stylish, sexy and in this case good enough to eat!

YOU WILL NEED

- 35 cm (14 in) square cake board
- 25 cm (10 in) round cake (see page 11)
- 550 g/1 lb 3½ oz/2¾ c buttercream (see page 8)
- Icing (confectioners') sugar in a sugar shaker
- Sugar glue and paintbrush
- Brown and black food colouring paste
- Boiled water, cooled

MODELLING PASTE (see page 10)

- 550 g (1 lb 3½ oz) black
- 90 g (3 oz) white
- 35 g (1¼ oz) cream

SUGARPASTE (see page 9)

- 750 g (1 lb 10½ oz) white
- 200 g (7 oz) cream
- 750 g (1 lb 10½ oz) dark pink

EQUIPMENT

- Shoe insole size UK4 EUR37 US6.5
- Roll of kitchen paper
- Sheet of paper
- Scissors
- Plain bladed kitchen knife
- Serrated carving knife
- Large rolling pin
- Cake smoother
- Palette knife
- Ruler
- No.2 sable paintbrush

Leave the sole to dry supported by the paper kitchen roll

1 Make the shoes first to allow plenty of drying time **(see left)**. Cut out a paper template using the shoe insole. Thickly roll out 400 g (14 oz) of black modelling paste and cut out the shape. Flip the template over and repeat for the second shoe. Thinly roll out the white modelling paste and cut out two more shapes as before, cutting the toe area of each straight. Stick these on top of the soles. Leave to firm for a few moments, position on the paper towel roll and then leave to dry.

2 Thinly roll out black modelling paste and cut two strips for the top of each shoe measuring 14 x 1.5 cm (5½ x ½ in) in length. Curve around to the width of each shoe and place each on their side to set for a few moments before sticking in position. Cut out four straps measuring 8 cm (3 in) in length, loop around and then stick in place at the back.

The heel shape stages

shoe leaving a little black showing. Thinly roll out black and cut two strips for each heel strap measuring 10 cm (4 in) in length and stick in position.

7 Thinly roll out the cream sugarpaste and cut a straight edge. Butt this straight edge up against the side of the cake, smooth with the cake smoother and then trim excess from around the cake board edge. Thinly roll out dark pink, gather up and cover the cake board up and around the cake. Secure with sugar glue and then trim excess from around the edge.

3 To make the heels, split 120 g (4¼ oz) of black modelling paste in half. Roll one half into a long teardrop shape and press down on the full end to flatten. Lay flat then smooth the heel until 10 cm (4 in) in length. Make the second heel. Leave both to set and then stand upside down and gently press each until at an angle **(see above)**.

4 Trim the crust from the cake and level the top. Cut the cake exactly in half. Cut a layer in each half. Spread buttercream on the underside of the bottom layer and position at an angle on the cake board. Sandwich the remaining layers together one on top of each other. Spread a thin layer over the surface of the cake as a crumb coat and to help the sugarpaste stick.

5 To keep sharp corners in the cake covering, measure the side of each cake carefully and cut pieces to fit. Apply the sugarpaste to the sides of the cake one piece at a time covering the opposite ends first **(see right)**. Roll up the cut pieces for the two long sides to prevent distortion, sticking the ends closed using a little

sugar glue. Use the cake smoother to gain a smooth neat surface. To make the box lid, roll out 340 g (12 oz) dark pink sugarpaste and cover the top of the cake and over the edge. Smooth around the shape and then trim excess.

6 Thinly roll out the cream modelling paste and cut two strips each measuring 14 x 2.5 cm (5½ x 1 in). Stick in place across each

8 Dilute black food colouring paste with water until a water colour paint consistency. Using the paintbrush, paint zebra stripes over the shoes and the box. Dilute brown and paint circles over the cream part of the board and across the shoes followed by black edging making the leopard print pattern. When the shoes are completely dry, stick the heels in position and then each shoe on top of the cake.

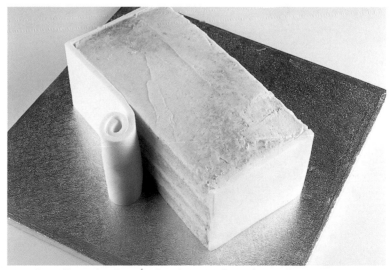

Gently roll up the long side piece and apply to the cake

Sexy Santa

I dressed this stunner in Santa clothing to make a fun alternative to the usual Christmas cake, but of course this design can easily be adapted for another celebration with some minor costume changes.

YOU WILL NEED

- 2 x 15 cm (6 in) square sponge cakes
- 25 cm (10 in) square cake board
- 550 g / 1 lb 3½ oz / 2¾ c buttercream (see page 11)
- Icing (confectioners') sugar in a sugar shaker
- Sugar glue and paintbrush
- Red and black food colouring paste

SUGARPASTE *(see page 9)*

- 370 g (13 oz) pale red
- 1.14 kg (2½ lb) white

MODELLING PASTE *(see page 10)*

- 115 g (4 oz) pale red
- 75 g (2½ oz) flesh
- 15 g (½ oz) white
- 5 g (just under ¼ oz) pale yellow
- 20 g (¾ oz) black

EQUIPMENT

- Plain-bladed kitchen knife
- Serrated carving knife
- Large and small rolling pins
- Ruler
- Cake smoother
- Palette knife
- A few cocktail sticks
- Small pieces of foam (for support)
- 1 x 30 cm (12 in) food-safe dowelling
- Miniature circle cutter
- Fine paintbrush

1 Slightly dampen the cake board with water. Roll out the red sugarpaste using a sprinkling of icing sugar and cover the cake board, trimming excess from around the edge. Set aside to dry.

2 Trim the crust from each cake and level the tops. Cut a layer in each cake and stack one on top of each other. Sandwich all layers together with buttercream. Spread buttercream on the underside of the cake, place centrally on the cake board and then spread a thin layer over the surface of the cake as a crumb coat and to help the paste stick.

3 Roll out 800 g (1 lb 12 oz) of white sugarpaste and cut a strip the height of the cake 60 cm (24 in) in length. Dust with icing sugar and then roll up lengthways. Position against the back of the cake and unroll around the cake, trimming excess away at join and smoothing closed with a little sugar glue. Rub in a circular motion to remove the join completely. Rub the surface with a cake smoother.

TIP: For a festive look, brush a tiny sprinkling of non-toxic food-safe glitter over the board.

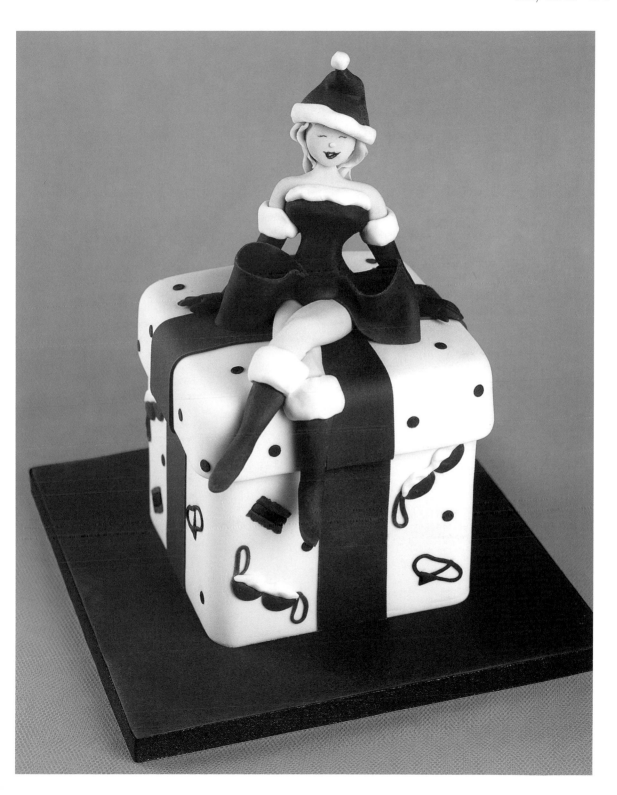

4 To make the box lid, roll out the remaining white sugarpaste and cover over the top of the cake and down the sides, cutting excess away and leaving a 4 cm (1½ in) lip **(see right)**. Using 30 g (1 oz) of red modelling paste, thinly roll out and cut the strips for the ribbon measuring 4 cm (1½ in) width. Cover the sides first, then the top.

5 To make the dress, roll 45 g (1½ oz) of pale red modelling paste into a sausage and indent around the centre to narrow the waist. Press down to flatten the stomach area and her back, keeping the chest area and her bottom rounded. Cut straight across the top and bottom of the dress and stick in place on the centre of the cake at a slight angle. Push the dowelling down through the body and into the cake, leaving 2.5 cm (1 in) protruding from the top of the dress.

6 To make the boots, split 20 g (¾ oz) of red modelling paste in half. Roll a sausage and bend one end round for the foot, pressing either side to narrow. Pinch the toe area to make it pointed. Pinch at the heel stroking it down to a point. Roll gently at the ankle to indent. Lay flat and cut the top straight **(see right)**. Repeat for the second boot.

7 For legs, split 45 g (1½ oz) of flesh in half and roll into tapering sausages, each measuring 5 cm (2 in) in length. Pinch gently halfway and push in at the back to indent the knees. Cut the top and bottom of each leg straight and stick in place, one crossed over the other, sticking the boots in place supported by the cake sides. Use foam pieces for support if necessary.

Making the box lid

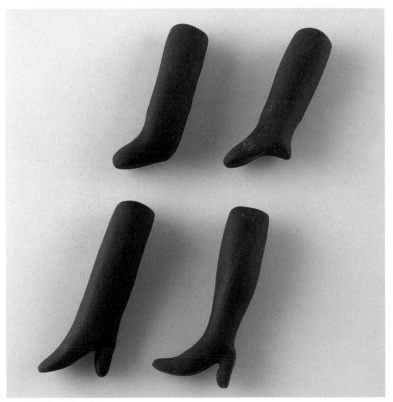

Modelling the boots

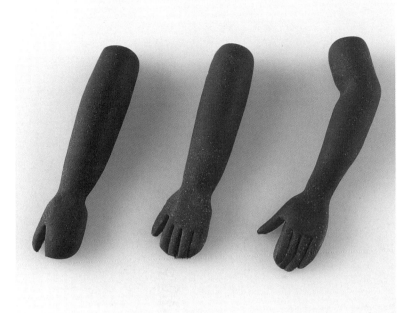

Modelling the gloves

Model a small bobble for the top of the hat. The hair is different sized flattened teardrop shapes of pale yellow modelling paste, built up little by little with the smaller pieces on top.

12 To make the bow, with 15 g (½ oz) of pale red, model two tapering sausage shapes and roll flat until the length measurement is around 10 cm (4 in). Mark pleats at both ends, moisten with glue and then fold over making two loops. Stick in place on the girl's lap with a small oval shape for the centre.

13 With the remaining white, red and black modelling paste make the bra, thong and garter for the box decoration, pressing each gently in place to inlay slightly using the cake smoother. Roll out black trimmings and cut the dots using the miniature circle cutter.

14 When the cake is dry, separately dilute black and red food colouring paste with a few drops of water. Using the fine paintbrush, paint her lips, eyes and eyelashes.

8 The shoulders, neck and top of each arm are modelled from 10 g (¼ oz) of flesh modelling paste first rolled into a sausage. Pinch the centre at the top to bring up a neck and stick in place over the dowelling, smoothing the chest area down and bending the two ends down for arms. If the shoulders become too rounded pinch back up to make more angular.

9 To make a glove, split 10 g (¼ oz) of pale red modelling paste in half and roll a sausage shape, pinching gently at one end to round off for a hand. Press either side of the hand to lengthen into an oval shape and press onto the top to flatten slightly, without indenting. Make a cut no further than halfway down on one side for the thumb. Make three slightly shorter cuts along the top to separate fingers and smooth gently to lengthen, then press together and bend round. To naturally shape the hand, push the thumb towards the palm from the wrist **(see above)**. Cut the end straight and stick in place on the arm resting on the top of the cake.

10 Make an oval-shaped head and ball nose using the remaining flesh modelling paste, flatten the face slightly and smooth down to create a ridge to outline the chin area, pinching in either side to shape the face. To make the hat, roll a 5 g (just under ¼ oz) teardrop of pale red modelling paste and hollow out the full end. Stick in place at a slight angle pinching up at the top and bending the point forward.

11 Using the white modelling paste, roll uneven sausage shapes to edge the top of each boot and glove, across her chest, along the bottom of the dress and around the hat, pinching up to texture the surface.

TIP: If you find the sugarpaste gloves are drying out before you have finished modelling them, moisten your fingertips with a tiny amount of water whilst you work.

Panties!

Sumptuous gold and black lace, lots of pretty bows and frills, what girl could resist this pile of handmade designer undies?

YOU WILL NEED

- 35 cm (14 in) round cake board
- 20 cm (8 in) round cake (see page 11)
- 450 g/1 lb/2 c buttercream (see page 8)
- Icing (confectioners') sugar in a sugar shaker
- Sugar glue and paintbrush
- Edible gold powdered food colouring

SUGARPASTE (see page 9)

- 1.2 kg (2 lb 10¼ oz) white

MODELLING PASTE (see page 10)

- 200 g (7 oz) pale pink
- 200 g (7 oz) white
- 200 g (7 oz) dark pink
- 200 g (7 oz) black

ROYAL ICING (see page 9)

- 30 g (1 oz) black

EQUIPMENT

- Plain bladed kitchen knife
- Serrated carving knife
- Large rolling pin
- Cake smoother
- Palette knife
- Ruler
- A few cocktail sticks
- Medium sized heart cutter
- Lace embosser, texture mat or lace piece
- No.1 plain piping tube (tip)
- Paper piping bag

1 Slightly dampen the cake board with water. Roll out the 500 g (1 lb 1¾ oz) white sugarpaste using a sprinkling of icing sugar and cover the cake board, trimming excess from around the edge. Set aside to dry.

2 Trim the crust from the cake and level the top. Cut two layers in the cake and sandwich back together with buttercream. Spread buttercream on the underside of the cake, place centrally on the cake board and then spread a thin layer over the surface of the cake as a crumb coat and to help the sugarpaste stick. Roll out the white sugarpaste and cover the cake

Gather up rolled out sugarpaste and position centrally

completely, smoothing down and around the shape trimming excess neatly from around the base. Rub the surface with a cake smoother. To give

height to the pile of panties, thinly roll out white trimmings and gather up into pleats, arranging centrally on top of the cake **(see left)**.

3 Use all the different coloured modelling paste to make the panties and thongs. To make a pair of panties, thinly roll out modelling paste and cut two strips each measuring 18 x 7 cm (7 x 3 in). Cut curved lines from the bottom up to the top edge to shape the front of one piece and then place this on top of the second strip sticking the corners and bottom with a little sugar glue. Use this top piece as a template and cut around making

Rub gold over the surface of the embossed lace to highlight the pattern

each leg area slightly larger. For the black and gold lace panties, indent the lace pattern first before cutting out the shape **(see left)**. Indent a pattern around the edge of some by pressing in with the end of a paintbrush.

4 To make a thong, thinly roll out paste and cut a strip measuring 25 x 7 cm (10 x 3 in). Cut out the leg areas as before making the top much thinner. Loop these opposite sides and stick together. Flip over to hide the join. The striped thong is made as before but using pale and dark pink paste kneaded together until streaky then stretched before rolling out to

make a striped effect. For lacing, thinly roll out paste and cut tiny strips criss-crossing them in place following indented holes made with the end of a paintbrush.

5 Decorate the panties and thongs with little bows made with thinly cut strips of modelling paste and looping each round. For the piped lace, pipe black royal icing in a filigree pattern. To pipe dots, squeeze gently to make small bulbs and then touch the top of each with a damp paintbrush to soften any points.

Camping Fun

This fun scene is reminiscent of young, free and easy camping days, and of course the nights... For rock festival fans you could add splashes of melted chocolate for a mud effect.

YOU WILL NEED

- 23 cm (9 in) and 20 cm (8 in) round sponge cakes (see page 11)
- 30 cm (12 in) round cake board
- 550 g / 1 lb 3½ oz / 2¾ c buttercream (see page 8)
- Icing (confectioners') sugar in a sugar shaker
- Sugar glue and paintbrush
- Edible silver lustre powder

SUGARPASTE *(see page 9)*

- 45 g (1½ oz) black
- 1.14 kg (2½ lb) purple
- 260 g (9 oz) green

MODELLING PASTE *(see page 10)*

- 35 g (1¼ oz) flesh
- 5 g (just under ¼ oz) blue
- 5 g (just under ¼ oz) purple
- 10 g (¼ oz) black

EQUIPMENT

- Plain-bladed kitchen knife
- Serrated carving knife
- Large rolling pin
- Cake smoother
- Palette knife
- New pan scourer (for texture)
- A few cocktail sticks
- Small pieces of foam (for support)

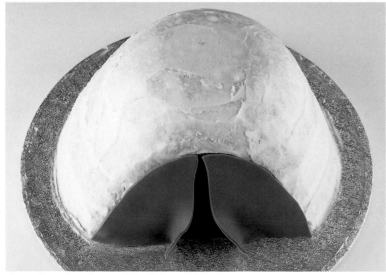

Covering the doorway with sugarpaste

1 Trim the crust from each cake and level the top of the larger cake only. Cut a layer in each cake and stack one on top of each other. Shape the sides of the cake to slope and round off. Cut away a slice from one side of the cake for the tent doorway. Sandwich all layers together with buttercream. Spread buttercream on the underside of the cake, place centrally on the cake board and then spread a thin layer over the surface of the cake as a crumb coat and to help the paste stick.

2 Thinly roll out the black sugarpaste and cover the doorway area following the arched shape (**see left**). Thinly roll out

45 g (1½ oz) purple and cut another piece the same size, cut in half and stick in position for the door flaps. Open up at the bottom and support until dry with foam pieces.

3 Roll out 900 g (2 lb) of purple sugarpaste and cover the cake completely, smoothing down and around the shape, trimming excess from around the doorway and smoothing gently to round off the cut edge. Trim excess from around the base. For grass, roll out the green sugarpaste into a long strip and stick over the cake board using a little sugar glue. For the textured grass effect, press the scourer into the surface repeatedly and then trim excess from around the edge of the cake board.

4 Thinly roll out the remaining purple sugarpaste and cut a strip for around the base of the cake measuring 55 x 6 cm (22 x 2¼ in), tapering slightly narrower towards both ends. Stick in position trimming excess from either side of the doorway. Thinly roll out the pink and cut an oblong measuring 27 x 15 cm (10½ x 6 in). Cut a curve lengthways from opposite sides and stick in place across the top of the tent.

5 To make a foot, first split the flesh modelling paste into four. Roll one piece into a sausage and bend half round for the foot, pinching up gently on the bottom to shape the heel and indent the arch of the foot. Pinch around the ankle. Cut toes, pinching up the large toe and stroke down the other toes so they curve underneath **(see right)**. Make three more feet and stick in position in the doorway.

6 Using blue modelling paste, shape two socks, hollowing out one and sticking in place over the top of a foot, pushing down gently and marking wrinkles with a knife. Thinly roll out white modelling paste and cut a strip to decorate the top of each sock. Shape the remaining white into a flattened square for the boxer shorts and pinch down two legs, hollowing each out slightly. Mark the fly and waistband using a knife.

7 For the torch, roll the mauve modelling paste into a teardrop and press down on the full end to flatten. Roll the back part into a sausage shaped handle and cut the end straight. Roll a small black sausage and indent rings by rolling a cocktail stick over the surface. Cut both ends straight and stick in place on the torch. For the light, rub a little silver powder over the surface.

8 Make the bra with the remaining black modelling paste. The main part is made from a fat sausage rolled gently in the centre to narrow. Stick down onto two separate long flattened teardrop-shaped straps and then stick in place on top of the tent.

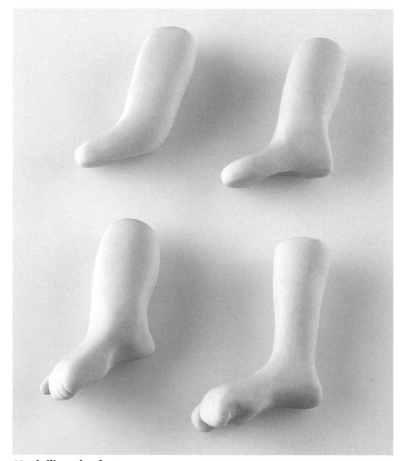

Modelling the feet

Saucy Stockings

This cheeky bottom complete with saucy black stockings and racy red bows is sure to create a lot of interest and cause a few heads to turn.

YOU WILL NEED

- 2 x 1-litre (2-pint) bowl-shaped sponge cakes (see page 11)
- 35-cm (14-in) round cake board
- 450 g / 1 lb / 2 c buttercream (see page 8)
- Icing (confectioners') sugar in a sugar shaker
- Sugar glue and paintbrush

SUGARPASTE (see page 9)

- 500 g (1 lb 1¾ oz) white
- 1.8 kg (4 lb) flesh

MODELLING PASTE (see page 10)

- 90 g (3 oz) black
- 90 g (3 oz) white
- 45 g (1½ oz) red

ROYAL ICING (see page 10)

- 15 g (½ oz) white

EQUIPMENT

- Plain-bladed kitchen knife
- Serrated carving knife
- Large and small rolling pins
- Cake smoother
- Palette knife
- A few cocktail sticks
- Ruler
- Small pieces of foam (for support)
- Paper piping bag
- No.1.5 plain piping tube

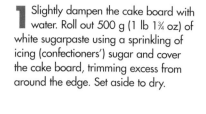

1 Slightly dampen the cake board with water. Roll out 500 g (1 lb 1¾ oz) of white sugarpaste using a sprinkling of icing (confectioners') sugar and cover the cake board, trimming excess from around the edge. Set aside to dry.

2 Trim the crust from each cake and level the tops. Slice away a wedge from each measuring 4 cm (1½ in) so they fit together neatly making the bottom shape. Cut two layers in each cake, sandwiching back together with buttercream. Spread buttercream on the underside of each cake and then place together centrally on the cake board. Spread a thin layer over the surface as a crumb coat and to help the paste stick, reserving some for later.

3 To pad out the legs, roll out 340 g (12 oz) of flesh-coloured sugarpaste into a wedge that is thick one end and thin the other. Press the thicker end up against the bottom and smooth down either side to narrow and shape the legs, smoothing the paste down to the cake board edge. Indent down the centre to separate the legs using the paintbrush handle. Trim excess away from around the cake board. Pad the back as legs, smoothing a narrow waistline using 340 g (12 oz) of flesh-colour (**see left**). Thickly spread the remaining buttercream at both joins to fill any dip and gain a smooth graduation ready for the sugarpaste covering.

4 Roll out the remaining flesh-colour and cover the cake, back and legs completely, smoothing around the shape and trimming excess away. Gently mark the bottom line and mark a line to separate the legs using the back of a knife, smoothing the line with your finger. Indent the spine using the paintbrush handle (**see above right**).

Forming the legs

Covering the cake, back and legs completely

7 Using the royal icing, pipe triangular shaped filigree along the bottom edge of the panties and then pipe a line of little dots edging across the top. Roll out red modelling paste and cut a strip to fit across the stocking tops measuring 2.5 cm (1 in) in depth. Press the paintbrush handle into the surface along the length, indenting two lines. Pinch gently to create folds and stick in place just below the stocking tops.

5 For stockings, roll out the black modelling paste as thinly as possible and cover the legs just below the bottom, following the curve of each cheek. Trim excess away and smooth down between each leg, securing with a little sugar glue. Roll the trimmings into a long thin sausage for the stocking tops and stick in place edging the top. Mark a line down the back of each stocking using the paintbrush handle.

6 Thinly roll out the white modelling paste and cut a strip for the panties 8 cm (3 in) in depth, measuring the width across the bottom and down the sides. From the base of the strip, cut curves from the centre out to each side so the panties taper down to a depth of 4 cm (1½ in) on either side. Using a little sugar glue to secure, stick in place **(see below)**.

8 For bows, first shape two flattened oval shapes for bow centres from pea sized amounts of red modelling paste and set aside. Split the remainder into four equally sized pieces. Roll one piece into a fat sausage and then roll gently at either end to bring to a point. Press down to flatten and smooth out, making the edge fine. Mark pleat lines from each point, radiating out to the centre, moisten the reverse with sugar glue at the point and then fold over making a loop. Make another loop and then stick together with a bow centre to complete the bow **(see below)**. Stick upright against the side of the stocking top. Repeat for the second bow.

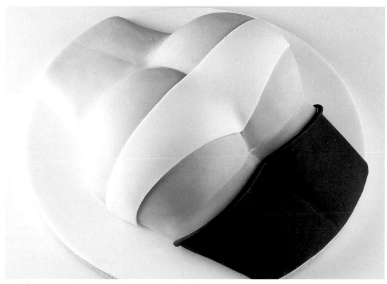

Sticking on the panties

Making the bows

Last Night of Freedom

It's certainly a bit of a giggle seeing the potential groom trussed up in this unenviable situation, but if you still want that invitation to the wedding, perhaps it's better in cake only!

YOU WILL NEED

- 23cm (9 in) and 20 cm (8 in) round sponge cakes (see page 11)
- 35cm (14in) round cake board
- 550 g / 1 lb 3½ oz / 2¾ c buttercream (see page 8)
- Icing (confectioners') sugar in a sugar shaker
- Sugar glue and paintbrush
- Spring green dusting powder

SUGARPASTE *(see page 9)*

- 550 g (1 lb 3½ oz) pale grey
- 650 g (1 lb 7 oz) pale green

MODELLING PASTE *(see page 10)*

- 5 g (just under ¼ oz) bright yellow
- 45 g (1½ oz) flesh
- 15 g (½ oz) red
- Pea-sized amount black
- 15 g (½ oz) white

ROYAL ICING *(see page 9)*

- 5 g (just under ¼ oz) cream

EQUIPMENT

- Plain-bladed kitchen knife
- Serrated carving knife
- Large and small rolling pins
- Cake smoother
- Palette knife
- A few cocktail sticks
- New pan scourer (for texture)
- 1 x 30 cm (12 in) food-safe dowelling
- Ball tool
- Small pieces of foam (for support)
- 3 cm (1¼ in) and 2.5 cm (1 in) circle cutters
- Medium paintbrush

1 Slightly dampen the cake board with water. Roll out 500 g (1 lb 1¾ oz) of the pale grey sugarpaste using a sprinkling of icing sugar and cover the cake board, trimming excess from around the edge. Set aside to dry.

2 Trim the crust from each cake and level the top of the larger cake only. Cut a layer in each cake and stack centrally one on top of each other. Shape the sides of the cake to round off into a dome shape and then sandwich all layers together with buttercream. Spread buttercream on the underside of the cake, place centrally on the cake board and then spread a thin layer over the surface of the cake as a crumb coat and to help the paste stick. Leave to set for around ten minutes to firm up. Rework the surface a little to soften the buttercream when ready to cover with sugarpaste.

TIP: You could omit the legs and position his body in a pile of 'dirt' made with textured brown modelling paste. It will look as though his party pals had a digger pour some dirt over him!

3 Roll out the pale green sugarpaste and cover the cake completely, smoothing around the shape and trimming excess from around the base. Texture the grass effect by pressing repeatedly over the surface with the scourer (**see right**).

4 To cover the dowelling for the lamppost, moisten the surface with sugar glue, roll out the remaining pale grey sugarpaste and then place the dowelling down onto it, wrapping the paste around and then smooth the join closed. Gently roll over the work surface to smooth and then cut excess from the bottom part so the covering sits level with the top of the cake. Push the dowelling down through the cake securing the base with a little sugar glue.

5 With grey trimmings, shape a flattened circle for the top of the lamppost and then roll three small balls for lights, indenting into the centre of each using a ball tool. Stick in place and fill each indent with tiny flattened balls of bright yellow.

6 Make the legs for the figure model using 15 g (½ oz) of flesh modelling paste split into two. To make a leg, roll one half into a sausage and bend one end for the foot, pinching up gently to shape the heel. Pinch around the ankle. Cut toes, pinching up the large toe and stroke down the other toes so they curve underneath. Lay the leg down and push in at the back halfway between the ankle and the top of the leg, pinching the front to shape the knee. Make the second leg and stick in position at the base of the lamppost.

Adding a grass effect texture

7 Make the body next by shaping a rounded teardrop with 15 g (½ oz) of flesh modelling paste and press down to flatten slightly. Pinch half way to indent the waist and round off the bottom. Pinch up a neck at the full end. Mark a line down the centre. Roll the paintbrush handle from the bottom up to gain excess for the pectorals, smoothing a curve on the underside of each and indenting with a cocktail stick.

8 For the arms, split the remaining flesh modelling paste into three equally sized pieces. Set one piece aside for the head later. To make an arm, roll into a sausage shape and pinch gently one end to round off a hand and narrow the wrist. Press the hand to flatten without indenting and then cut a thumb on one side no further than half way. Make three more cuts along the top cutting one-third from the top and smooth the fingers round to curve the hand naturally. Push the thumb down towards the palm from the wrist. Push in halfway along the arm, pinching out at the back to shape the elbow. Stick in place bent backwards and stuck to the lamppost with palm uppermost. Make the second arm in the same way, crossing the hands over at the back. Add a little more glue to the join at each shoulder and gently smooth the joins closed.

9 Model an oval-shaped head, nose and ears using the piece of flesh modelling paste set aside earlier, indenting his open mouth by pressing in with the end of a paintbrush and pulling gently downwards to encourage a full bottom lip. For the closed eyes, first indent two small holes using the end of a paintbrush, and then for eyelids, model a minute

Modelling the head and face

cut strips to cover around the centre of each cone. Stick one cone on the man's head, supported by the lamppost.

12 Using the remaining white, thinly roll out and cut strips and triangle shapes for the road markings, and then cut long strips of white for the tape, wrapping repeatedly around the figure and lamppost. Thinly roll out the remaining red and cut tiny stripes for the tape. Stick the road sign in place.

13 Put the royal icing into a piping bag, cut a small hole in the tip and pipe the hair. Mix a little green powder and icing sugar together and then dust the grass around the figure and around the base of the cake using the medium paintbrush.

oval of flesh modelling paste and press flat. Cut in half widthways and use the straight edge for the bottom of each eye **(see above)**. Cut a little from the top of his head at an angle so the cone 'hat' will sit straight and then stick in place resting against the lamppost.

gently to straighten completely. For bases, roll out and cut three circles using the small circle cutter and then cut around the edge of each making them angular. Stick the cones centrally on each base with a tiny ball of red on the top. Thinly roll out white and

10 To make the road sign, thinly roll out a little red modelling paste and cut out a circle using the largest cutter. Roll out yellow and cut another circle using the smallest cutter. Roll out black modelling paste as thinly as possible and cut a strip for the centre of the road sign, sticking in place on the yellow circle with a small cut out triangle for the arrow on the end. Cut the yellow circle in half then trim a little further so the resulting two half circles seat neatly on the red circle with a red diagonal strip showing and an even red ring around the outside **(see right)**.

11 To make the cones, split 10 g (¼ oz) of red into three and model teardrop shapes, pressing the rounded end of each down on the work surface to flatten. Roll the sides

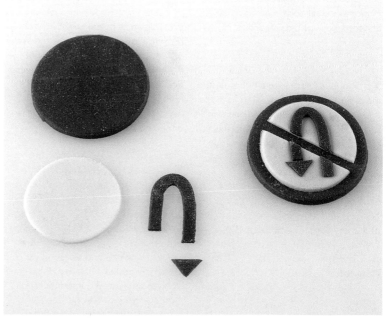

Assembling the road sign

Sexy Basque

This cake is quite an eye popper with the basque seemingly pulled in so tight. One way to gain an hourglass figure I suppose, unless you decide to eat more than a small slice of course!

YOU WILL NEED

- 2 x 1 litre (2 pint) bowl-shaped sponge cakes (see page 11)
- 45 cm (18 in) round cake board
- 450 g / 1 lb / 2 c buttercream (see page 8)
- Icing (confectioners') sugar in a sugar shaker
- Sugar glue and paintbrush

SUGARPASTE *(see page 9)*

- 800 g (1 lb 12 oz) black
- 1kg (2 lb 3¼ oz) flesh
- 1 kg (2 lb 3¼ oz) lilac

EQUIPMENT

- Plain-bladed kitchen knife
- Serrated carving knife
- Large rolling pin
- Ruler
- Cake smoother
- Palette knife
- A few cocktail sticks
- No.4 plain piping tube
- Miniature circle cutter

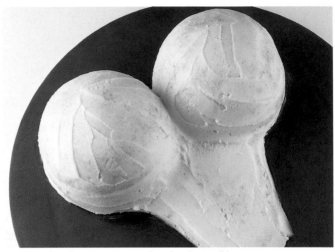

Sculpted cake on covered cake board

1 Slightly dampen the cake board with water. Roll out the black sugarpaste using a sprinkling of icing sugar and cover the cake board, trimming excess from around the edge. Reserve trimmings and set aside to dry.

2 Trim the crust from each cake and level the tops. Cut a layer in each cake and sandwich back together with buttercream. Spread buttercream on the underside of each cake and position on the cake board. Use the cake trimmings to raise the stomach area, slicing down at an angle until level with the cake board. Spread a thin layer of buttercream over the surface of the cake as a crumb coat and to help the paste stick **(see above)**.

3 Roll out the flesh sugarpaste and cover the boobs completely, smoothing around the shape and covering up to the top of the cake board. Trim a curve around the top and trim excess from around the sides of the boobs, smoothing the sugarpaste down over the stomach until completely level with the cake board surface.

4 For the basque, roll out the lilac sugarpaste around 2-3 mm thickness and half cover the boobs down to the bottom of the cake board. Smooth around the shape and trim a straight line across the top of the cake and a curved line at the bottom leaving a 1 cm (½ in) space from the cake board edge. Gently push the

Cutting the sugarpaste to fit

sugarpaste into the cleavage and then make a small cut. From this small cut, indent a line all the way down the centre. Trim either side to narrow the waist and shape the hips, smoothing the sugarpaste to round off and create a 3D effect **(see left)**. Cut out eyelet holes down the centre on either side using the piping tube.

5 With lilac trimmings, cut thin strips to decorate the basque for the 'boned' effect. Thinly roll out and cut small circles with the miniature circle cutter, cutting each in half and use to edge the basque at the top and bottom. Thinly roll out the black trimmings and cut small strips to slot into the eyelet holes, criss-crossing from the bottom upwards. Cut longer strips for the opening at the top.

Centerfold

This cake certainly has the 'wow' factor with a scantily dressed blonde spread out provocatively in a magazine centerfold.

YOU WILL NEED

- 30 x 25 cm (12 x 10 in) oblong shaped sponge cake (see page 11)
- 35 cm (14 in) square cake board
- 550 g / 1 lb 3½ oz / 2¾ c buttercream (see page 8)
- Icing (confectioners') sugar in a sugar shaker
- Sugar glue and paintbrush
- Blue, pink, black and red food colouring paste
- 1–2 tsp water

SUGARPASTE (see page 9)

- 500 g (1 lb 1¾ oz) mid blue
- 1 kg (2 lb 3¼ oz) pale blue

MODELLING PASTE (see page 10)

- 1.14 kg (2½ lb) white
- 225 g (½ lb) flesh

ROYAL ICING (see page 9)

- 30 g (1 oz) deep cream

EQUIPMENT

- Plain-bladed kitchen knife
- Serrated carving knife
- Large rolling pin
- Cake smoother
- Palette knife
- A4 sheet of paper or similar
- Ruler
- A few cocktail sticks
- Foam pieces (for support)
- Medium and fine paintbrushes
- Paint palette

1 Slightly dampen the cake board with water. Roll out the mid blue sugarpaste using a sprinkling of icing sugar and cover the cake board. Press the rolling pin over the surface to create a rippled effect, trim excess from around the edge and then set aside to dry.

2 Trim the crust from the cake and level the top. Trim off the top and bottom edge. Cut two layers in the cake and sandwich back together with buttercream. Spread buttercream on the underside of the cake, place on the cake board at a slight angle and then spread a thin layer over the surface of the cake as a crumb coat and to help the sugarpaste stick. Leave to set for around ten minutes to firm up. Rework the surface a little to soften the buttercream when ready to cover with sugarpaste.

TIP: Add a painted magazine style heading with a message for the recipient using diluted black food colouring paste and a fine paintbrush.

3 For the pillow fold, roll out 285 g (10 oz) of pale blue sugarpaste and cover one end of the cake, folding onto the top and then smooth the ridge until level with the cake surface **(see right)**. To make the pillow, roll out the remaining pale blue and cut a straight edge, covering the cake with this straight edge at the fold. Trim excess and tuck covering underneath around the cake. Roll the mid blue trimmings into a long thin sausage and stick in place for piping across the pillow.

4 To make the magazine, thinly roll out 225 g (½ lb) of white modelling paste and using the sheet of paper as a template, cut around. Place on the cake at a slight angle and support the corners using foam pieces until dry. Repeat four times and then using a ruler, mark down the centre for the magazine fold.

5 Dilute blue and pink food colouring separately with a little water until it is a watercolour consistency. Paint a streaked effect with blue leaving patches of white showing through. Keep the colour pale otherwise it will detract from the figure. Add a little pink to the paintbrush a little at a time and paint more streaks. The mix of blue and pink will add a mauve shade also **(see right)**. For the pillow, roll 60 g (2 oz) of white into an oval shape and pinch out four corners.

6 For the figure, roll 85 g (2¾ oz) of flesh modelling paste into a fat sausage and then roll between your thumb and finger to indent the waist half way, rounding off the bottom. Roll the opposite end to lengthen the chest area and pinch up gently at the top to round off the neck. Press the front flat and then bend backwards to create an arch in the back. Indent the belly button with the end of a paintbrush.

Creating the pillow fold

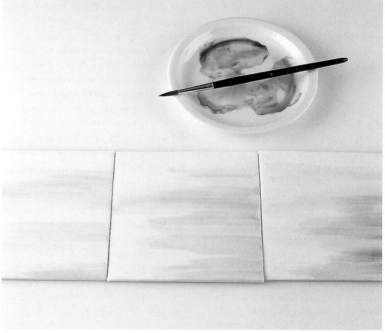

Painting the background

Modelling the figure

7 For her boobs, split 15 g (½ oz) of flesh modelling paste in half and roll both into teardrop shapes. Stick in place, smoothing up at each point to blend into the surface of the body and remove the join completely **(see above)**. Stick a tiny ball on each and then stick the body onto the cake with the neck resting at the bottom of the pillow.

8 For her legs, split 85 g (2¾ oz) of flesh modelling paste in half. Roll one half into a sausage. Bend one end round to make a foot, pinching gently to shape a heel. Roll the ankle area between your thumb and finger to indent and shape the leg. Push in half way up at the back and gently pinch at the front to shape the knee. Stroke the shin to straighten, pushing out excess at the back to shape the calf muscle. Bend in position and stick in place. Make the second leg in the same way but straighten out, pointing the toe. Use foam pieces to support in the pose until dry.

9 For her arms, split 20 g (¾ oz) of flesh modelling paste in half. To make the outstretched arm, roll a piece into a sausage shape and pinch gently one end to round off for a hand. Press down on the hand to flatten only slightly, without indenting. Make a cut half way down on one side for the thumb. Make three cuts along the top to separate fingers and twist gently to lengthen, press together and bend round. To naturally shape the hand, push the thumb towards the palm from the wrist. Lay the arm down and push in half way, pinching out at the back to shape the elbow.

10 The second arm is behind the girl's head, so the hand doesn't need to be finely modelled as it will be hidden. Make the second arm, bending it sharply at the elbow so the hand area rests just beyond the neck, and then stick in place, smoothing the join into the body.

11 For her head, roll 20 g (¾ oz) of flesh modelling paste into an oval shape, smoothing the facial area flat. Stick a tiny ball nose just below the centre. Stick her head in place supported by her hand resting on the pillow. Stick the remaining flesh behind her head to help support the hair.

12 Thinly roll out 90 g (3 oz) of white modelling paste and cut a square measuring around 15 cm (6 in). Gently fold into pleats and drape over the centre of her body. Repeat with the remaining white, pinching different sized rolled out pieces into drapes and folds and smoothing the joins into the surface of the magazine using a little sugar glue. Repeat to cover her boobs **(see below)**.

Folding the drapes

13 For her hair, put the royal icing into the piping bag and cut a small hole in the tip. Pipe her hair in waves starting at the back and spreading it over the pillow. Build up little by little with shorter lengths on top of her head at the front. When the cake is dry, dilute a little black and red food colouring separately with a few drops of water. Using the fine paintbrush paint her eyes, eyebrows and mouth.

Hot Boxers

This cheeky pair of boxer shorts decorated with funky hearts are not only extremely quick and simple to make but will make a great talking point for any celebration.

YOU WILL NEED

- 35 cm (14 in) square cake board
- 25 cm (10 in) square cake (see page 11)
- 450 g/1 lb/2 c buttercream (see page 8)
- Icing (confectioners') sugar in a sugar shaker
- Sugar glue and paintbrush

SUGARPASTE (see page 9)

- 800 g (1 lb 12 oz) black
- 1 kg (2 lb 3¼ oz) white
- 145 g (5 oz) red

EQUIPMENT

- Ruler
- Plain bladed kitchen knife
- Serrated carving knife
- Large rolling pin
- Cake smoother
- Palette knife
- A few cocktail sticks
- Medium sized heart cutter

1 Slightly dampen the cake board with water. Roll out the black sugarpaste using a sprinkling of icing sugar and cover the cake board, trimming excess from around the edge. Set aside to dry.

Position the shaped cake on the cake board

2 Trim the crust from the cake keeping the rounded top where the cake has risen. From the top edge of the cake, trim 2.5 cm (1 in) from either side to narrow the sides so they slope down and outwards to the bottom. Cut a wedge of cake centrally from the bottom edge 8 cm (3 in) in length to separate the legs **(see above)**.

3 Cut a layer in the cake, spread the underside of the bottom layer with buttercream and place centrally on the cake board. Sandwich the next layer on top using buttercream and then spread a thin layer over the surface of the cake as a crumb coat and to help the sugarpaste stick.

4 Roll out the white sugarpaste and cover the cake, smoothing around the shape and trimming excess from around the edge. Pinch around the waistband area and the bottom of each leg. Mark pleats by pressing in with the rolling pin. Indent a seam line down the centre using the back of a knife.

5 With white trimmings, cut a strip for the fly measuring 14 cm (5½ in) in length. Roll out the red sugarpaste and cut a strip for the waistband marking pleats with the back of a knife. Thinly roll out red trimmings and cut out hearts to decorate the boxers. Mark stitching with the tip of a cocktail stick **(see below)**.

Mark stitching with a cocktail stick

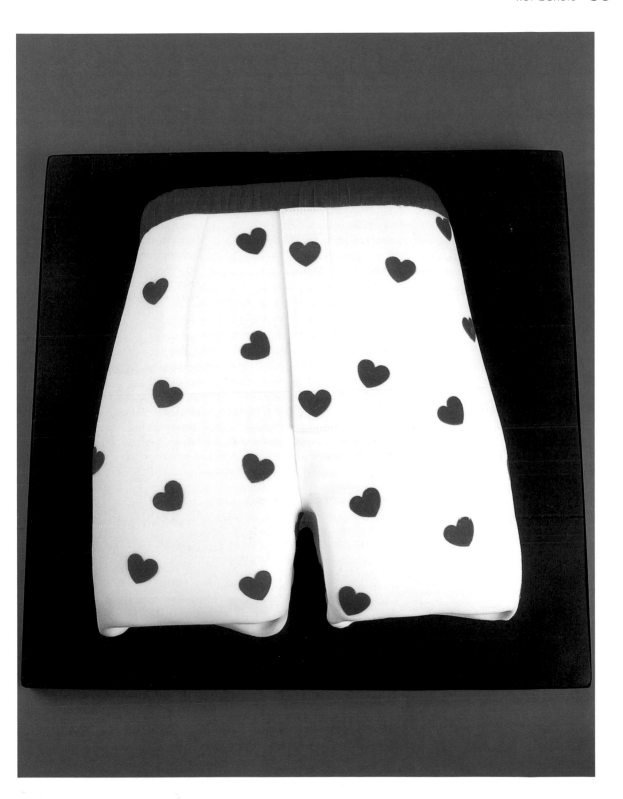

Builder's Bum

We've all had a giggle at workmen bending over and flashing a little too much, it makes the day much more interesting! Now you can show your appreciation with this fine specimen.

YOU WILL NEED

- 25 cm (10 in) round sponge cake (see page 11)
- 35 cm (14 in) round cake board
- 550 g / 1 lb 3½ oz / 2¾ c buttercream (see page 8)
- Icing (confectioners') sugar in a sugar shaker
- Sugar glue and paintbrush
- Edible silver powder
- 1–2 tsp clear alcohol (e.g. vodka, gin)
- Brown powdered food colouring

SUGARPASTE (see page 9)

- 500 g pale brown
- 1 kg (2 lb 3¼ oz) flesh
- 330 g (11½ oz) blue
- 60 g (2 oz) white

PASTILLAGE (see page 10)

- 60 g (2 oz) pale grey

MODELLING PASTE (see page 10)

- 100 g (3½ oz) pale brown
- 10 g (¼ oz) black

EQUIPMENT

- Plain-bladed kitchen knife
- 3.5 cm (1½ in) and 2.5 cm (1 in) circle cutters
- Serrated carving knife
- Large and small rolling pins
- Ruler
- Cake smoother
- Palette knife
- A few cocktail sticks
- Small pieces of foam (for support)
- Medium and fine paintbrushes

1 Slightly dampen the cake board with water. Roll out the pale brown sugarpaste using a sprinkling of icing sugar and cover the cake board, trimming excess from around the edge. Set aside to dry.

2 Make the tools first to allow for drying time. To make the ruler, thinly roll out 25 g (1 oz) of grey pastillage and cut a strip measuring 23 cm (9 in) in length. Mark measurement lines down both sides using a knife. For the hammer handle, roll 20 g (¾ oz) of grey pastillage into a sausage measuring 18 cm (7 in) in length and lay flat to dry.

TIP: Trim the bum to suit the recipient. The cake would look just as fun decorated for a window cleaner with a cloth hanging out of a pocket, or add a small rake or spade for a gardener.

3 To make the spanner, roll out the remaining grey pastillage and cut a strip for the handle measuring 8 cm (3 in) in length, tapering the width slightly. For the top, cut out a circle using the 3.5 cm (1½ in) cutter and

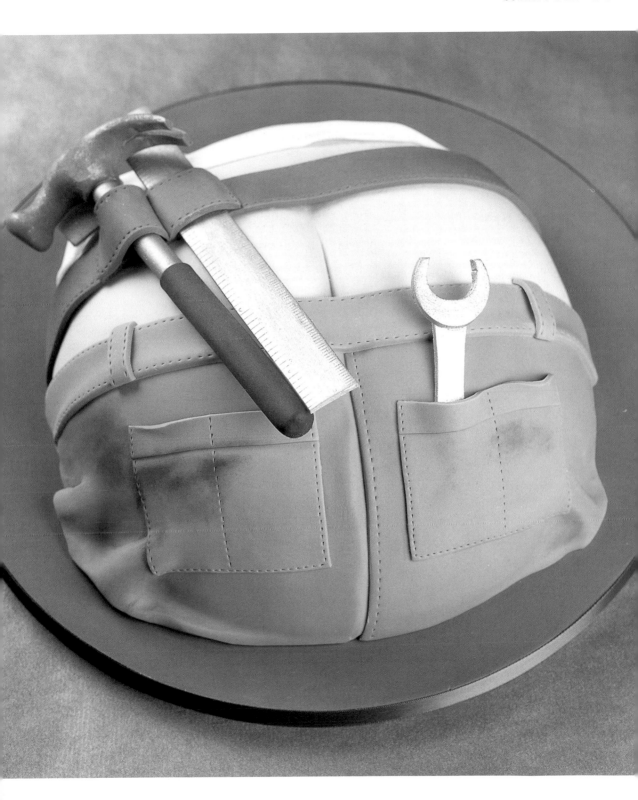

then from the top of this circle cut out a further circle using the 2.5 cm (1 in) cutter. Open the circle up a little, trim across the top and then stick onto the handle **(see right)**.

4 Dilute the edible silver with clear alcohol for a paint consistency. Apply a thin coat over the top of the ruler, spanner and hammer handle, leave to dry, turn over and paint the reverse. Repeat adding 2-3 thin coats until completely silver in colour.

5 To make the hammer head, following the step picture as a guide **(see right)**, roll 35 g (1¼ oz) of pale brown modelling paste into a fat sausage and then pinch in the centre on the underside bringing down excess to meet the handle. Push in the handle to make a hole, and then remove. Roll one end and then flatten and smooth the opposite end until tapered, making a cut for the claw. Open the claw slightly and then bend gently round. Set aside to dry.

Making the spanner

6 When the hammer handle is completely dry, thinly roll out black modelling paste and cover the bottom part of the handle, smoothing the join closed and trimming excess at the top. Stick the hammer head in place and then set aside.

7 Trim the crust from the cake leaving the rounded top where the cake has risen. Cut two layers in the cake and sandwich together with buttercream, filling the centre a little more to help shape the cake. Spread buttercream on the underside of the cake, place centrally on the cake board and then spread a thin layer over the surface of the cake as a crumb coat and to help the sugarpaste stick.

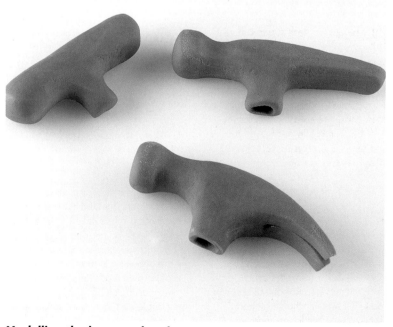

Modelling the hammer head

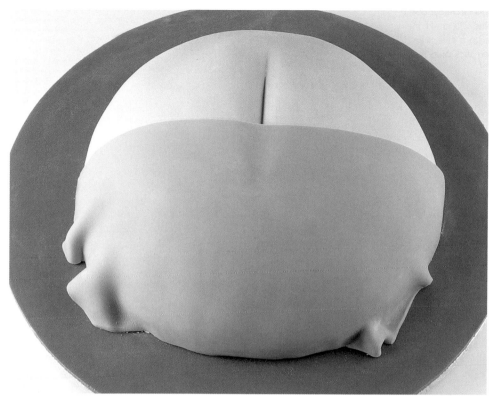

Creating pleats in the jeans

8 Roll out the flesh sugarpaste and cover the cake completely, smoothing around the shape and trimming excess from around the edge. Use the back of a knife to push the sugarpaste underneath around the base. Mark the crease on top of the cake by pressing in gently with the side of a ruler at an angle, turn and press the opposite side.

9 For the jeans, thinly roll out 225 g (½ lb) blue sugarpaste and cover the bottom part of the cake, securing with sugar glue. Encourage pleats for wrinkles down opposite sides **(see above)**. Mark down the centre using the flat of the ruler. Roll out 45 g (1½ oz) and cut a strip for the waistband. Use trimmings for belt loops, indenting the stitching with the tip of a knife.

10 Roll out the remaining blue sugarpaste and cut two pockets measuring 9 x 7 cm (3½ x 2¾ in). Mark a line across the top of each by pressing in with the flat of a ruler and stick in place, leaving one pocket open for the spanner. Indent the stitching down the centre of each pocket and around the edge.

11 Thinly roll out the white sugarpaste and cut a strip to cover the top of the cake for the t-shirt, encouraging wrinkles and pleats, and then trim away excess. For the belt, roll out and cut a strip using 45 g (1½ oz) brown modelling paste. Stick in place just below the t-shirt at a slight angle and then mark stitching.

12 Secure the tools onto the belt with a little sugar glue, supported by foam pieces. Roll out the remaining brown modelling paste and cut a further strip for the belt loop. Stick in place over the hammer and ruler, indenting into the centre and marking stitching as before.

13 To make the jeans look dirty, mix a little brown powdered food colouring with a sprinkling of icing sugar and brush onto the jeans in patches using the medium paintbrush. Stipple a little diluted edible silver over the surface of the hammer head.

Pierced Tongue

Bring out the rebel in you and make a statement with these fun lips and a big red pierced tongue.

YOU WILL NEED

- 1 x 30 cm (12 in) square sponge cake (see page 11)
- 45 cm (18 in) round cake board
- 450 g / 1 lb / 2 c buttercream (see page 8)
- Icing (confectioners') sugar in a sugar shaker
- Sugar glue and paintbrush
- 1 x sugar stick (see page 10)
- Edible silver powder
- A few drops of clear alcohol (e.g. vodka, gin)

SUGARPASTE (see page 9)

- 800 g (1 lb 12 oz) black
- 1.4 kg (3 lb 1½ oz) pale red

EQUIPMENT

- Plain-bladed kitchen knife
- Serrated carving knife
- Large rolling pin
- Cake smoother
- Palette knife
- Ruler
- A few cocktail sticks
- Medium paintbrush

1 Slightly dampen the cake board with water. Roll out the black sugarpaste using a sprinkling of icing sugar and cover the cake board, trimming excess from around the edge. Set aside to dry.

2 Trim the crust from the cake and level the top. Cut the cake exactly in half and stack one on top of the other. The tongue should be slightly narrower and lower at the back and fuller at the front. To shape the tongue, trim from the centre of the cake to slope back cutting down to 2 cm (¾ in). Use this trimming to pad out the front of the cake making it slightly fuller. Trim around the whole cake to round off. Trim a small 'v' from the back. Sandwich the layers together with buttercream. Spread buttercream

on the underside of the cake, place centrally on the cake board and then spread a thin layer over the surface of the cake as a crumb coat and to help the paste stick **(see below)**.

3 Roll out 1.2 kg (2 lb 10¼ oz) of red sugarpaste and cover the cake completely. Smooth around the shape, trimming excess from around the edge and tucking underneath. Rub the surface gently with a cake smoother. Using a ruler, mark down the centre from the back by pressing gently with the side of a ruler at an angle, turn and repeat on the opposite side to gain a neat indent with smooth sides.

Carving the tongue

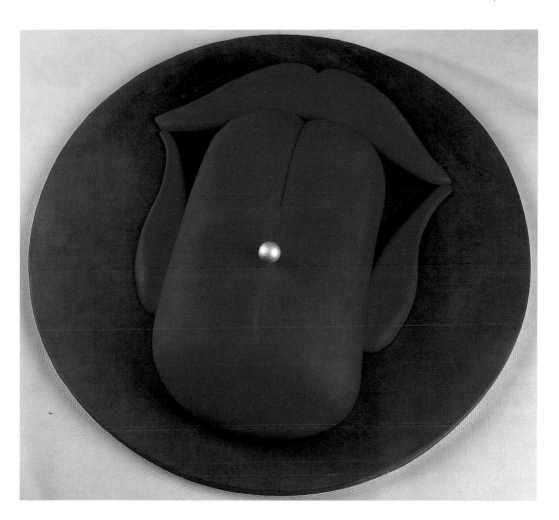

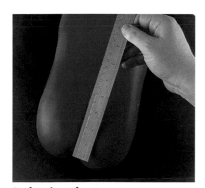

Indenting the tongue

4 For the top lip, roll 125 g (4½ oz) of red into a sausage 25 cm (10 in) in length, tapering to a point at each end. Gently roll flat using the rolling pin, bend the two sides down then curve up at each end. Indent a 'v' in the centre at the top using a ruler **(see left)** and then position on the cake board securing with a little sugar glue.

5 Split the remaining red in half and use to make the bottom lip on either side. Roll these pieces into identical teardrop shapes around 17 cm (6½ in) in length. Roll flat as

before and stick in place either side of the tongue with the point of each teardrop curving outwards at the top and meeting the corners of the top lip.

6 Moisten the sugar stick with a little sugar glue and push down into the centre of the tongue. To make the tongue ball, roll a ball of black trimmings and stick onto the sugar stick. Dilute a little edible silver powder with a few drops of clear alcohol and mix until a thick brushing paste. Paint a thin layer over the tongue ball and supporting sugar stick, leave to dry and then paint a further thin coat.

Wild West Dancers

This set of gorgeous frilled petticoats swirling around flashing sexy legs and underwear will be a great talking point at any celebration, or just make your favourite as a special individual treat.

YOU WILL NEED

- 6 x 10 cm (4 in) round sponge cakes (see page 11)
- 6 x 10 cm (4 in) round cake cards
- 550 g / 1 lb 3½ oz / 2¾ c buttercream (see page 8)
- Icing (confectioners') sugar in a sugar shaker
- Sugar glue and paintbrush
- Black food colouring paste

SUGARPASTE (see page 9)

- 900 kg (2 lb) white

MODELLING PASTE (see page 10)

- 60 g (2 oz) black
- 20 g (¾ oz) lilac
- 30 g (1 oz) royal blue
- 45 g (1½ oz) white
- 30 g (1 oz) orange
- 30 g (1 oz) red
- 30 g (1 oz) green
- 30 g (1 oz) yellow
- 75 g (2½oz) flesh

EQUIPMENT

- Plain-bladed kitchen knife
- Serrated carving knife
- Large and small rolling pins
- Cake smoother
- Palette knife
- A few cocktail sticks
- 10 cm (4 in), 9 cm (3½ in), 8 cm (3 in) and 6 cm (2½ in) circle cutters
- Fine paintbrush

1 Trim the crust from each cake and level the tops. Cut a layer in each cake and sandwich back together with buttercream. Spread buttercream on the underside of each cake and position on a cake card. Spread a thin layer of buttercream over the surface of each cake as a crumb coat and to help the sugarpaste stick.

2 To cover a cake, roll out 150 g (5¼ oz) of white sugarpaste and cover completely, smoothing down and around the shape, trimming excess from around the base. Smooth the surface with a cake smoother.

3 Using the circle cutters and all the coloured modelling paste, make all the frilled petticoats. As you apply a smaller circle to the top of a cake, position it slightly higher so the body can sit centrally on the smallest frill. To make a frill, thinly roll out modelling paste, cut a circle and then roll the paintbrush handle over the outside edge to thin and frill **(see right)**.

4 The legs and bottoms are modelled separately and the join disguised with a stocking top. To make a leg, split 10 g (¼ oz) of flesh modelling paste and roll one piece into a sausage. Bend one end round

Making the frilly petticoats

to make a foot, pinching gently to shape the rounded heel. Roll the ankle area between your thumb and finger to indent and shape the leg. Push in half way down at the back and gently pinch at the front to shape the knee.

Forming the legs and bottom

Stroke the shin to straighten, pushing out excess at the back to shape the calf muscle. Point the toe by stroking gently downwards and then cut the top straight in the centre of the thigh **(see above)**. For the bottom, roll a 5 g

(just under ¼ oz) sausage of flesh modelling paste measuring 4 cm (1½ in) and bend in the centre. Cut both ends straight and then stick legs in place. Thinly roll out modelling paste and cut thin strips to cover each join.

5 To make a shoe, roll a small pea-sized amount into a sausage and indent two thirds of the way down by rolling backwards and forwards with the paintbrush handle. Press down to flatten and stick in place following the contours of the bottom of the foot. Add a little teardrop shaped heel. Add heels to the boots.

6 The panties are thinly rolled out triangular shapes and when stuck in place the centre is indented with a cocktail stick. Cut thin strips for trimmings, looping round for bows and for frilled edging indent with the end of a paintbrush. Dilute black colouring with a few drops of water and paint very fine lines in a criss-cross pattern for fishnet stockings using the fine paintbrush. For plain stockings add a very tiny strip of black modelling paste down the centre of each leg.

Pin-up Girl

Older men can be notoriously difficult to make cakes for, but this stars and stripes sweetheart is certain to bring a little nostalgia to the celebration.

YOU WILL NEED

- 14 in round cake board
- 8 in round sponge cake (see page 11)
- 450 g / 1 lb / 2 c buttercream (see page 8)
- Icing (confectioners') sugar in a sugar shaker
- Sugar glue and paintbrush
- 1 x sugar stick (see page 10)
- 2 x paper piping bags
- Black food colouring paste

SUGARPASTE (see page 9)

- 500 g (1lb 1¾ oz) blue
- 800 g (1 lb 12 oz) white

MODELLING PASTE (see page 10)

- 110 g (3¾ oz) red
- 85 g (2¾ oz) white
- 60 g (2 oz) blue
- 20 g (¾ oz) flesh

ROYAL ICING (see page 10)

- 15 g (½ oz) white
- 20 g (¾ oz) cream

EQUIPMENT

- Plain-bladed kitchen knife
- Serrated carving knife
- Large and small rolling pins
- Ruler
- Cake smoother
- Palette knife
- A few cocktail sticks
- 5 cm (2 in) circle cutter
- Small pieces of foam (for support)
- 1 x 30 cm (12 in) food-safe dowelling
- Small and miniature star cutters
- Scissors
- Fine paintbrush

1 Slightly dampen the cake board with water. Roll out the blue sugarpaste using a sprinkling of icing sugar and cover the cake board, trimming excess from around the edge. Set aside to dry.

2 Trim the crust from the cake and level the top. Cut two layers in the cake and sandwich back together with buttercream. Spread buttercream on the underside of the cake, place centrally on the cake board and then spread a thin layer over the surface of the cake as a crumb coat and to help the paste stick. Leave to set for around ten minutes to firm up. Rework the surface a little to soften the buttercream when ready to cover with sugarpaste.

TIP: A quick and simple alternative to cut down on modelling is to wrap a large decorated flag around the figure so only the girl's top half is on show.

Covering the cake with sugarpaste

3 Roll out the white sugarpaste and cover the cake completely, smoothing around the shape and trimming excess from around the base **(see above)**. Rub the surface with a cake smoother. Thinly roll out 100 g (3½ oz) red and 45 g (1½ oz) white modelling paste and using a ruler, cut the stripes for around the base of the cake, smoothing the join closed with a little sugar glue.

4 Thinly roll out 35 g (1¼ oz) of blue modelling paste and cut out the stars to decorate around the cake and cut out the circle for the top using the circle cutter. Moisten the dowelling with a little sugar glue and place onto rolled out white modelling paste. Wrap the paste around the dowelling and smooth the join closed. Roll over the work surface to smooth the surface. Trim excess level with the top

of the cake and then push down into the cake, securing the base with a little sugar glue.

5 Roll out 5 g (¼ oz) of white modelling paste, cut a rectangle measuring 6 x 5 cm (2½ x 2 in) and then cut into a long triangular shaped flag. Stick in place wrapped around the top of the flagpole, holding for a minute until secure. With white trimmings, model a flattened ball for the top of the pole, then a smaller ball, and finally a small dome shape.

6 The figure is built up flat and then positioned when dry. For the boots, split 5 g (just under ¼ oz) of red modelling paste in half. To make a boot, roll a sausage and bend one end round for the foot, pressing either side to narrow. Pinch at the heel and

roll gently at the ankle to indent. Lay flat and cut the top straight. Repeat for the second boot and stick both boots together with toes slightly turned out.

7 For legs, split 10 g (¼ oz) of flesh in half and roll into tapering sausages, each measuring 5 cm (2 in) in length. Pinch gently halfway and push in at the back to indent the knees. Stick the legs together, and then cut the top and bottom of each straight, sticking in place on the boots **(see above right)**.

8 To make the body, roll 20 g (¾ oz) of blue modelling paste into a sausage and indent around the centre to narrow the waist. Press down to flatten front and back and pinch up a neck. Cut the bottom straight and stick in place on the legs. Roll these

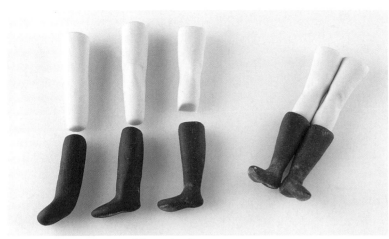

Modelling and assembling the legs

slightly smaller square for the centre of the red buckle. Thinly roll out the remaining blue and cut a tiny strip to edge underneath the chest and over the joins at each shoulder. Make the hat with the remaining white by shaping a flattened circle for the top, pinching it up at the front. Model a tiny tapering sausage for the front and make a small semi-circle for the peak.

12 When the figure is completely dry, dilute black colouring with a tiny amount of water and paint the eyes with the fine paintbrush. Make sure the brush has minimal colour on it to keep the lines very fine. Any painted mistakes can be wiped away with a clean brush.

13 Pipe a line of white royal icing along the front of the flagpole and press the figure against it, holding for a few seconds until secure. Put the cream royal icing into a piping bag and cut a small hole in the tip. Pipe the girl's wavy hair, building up around the back of her head, her shoulders and against the flagpole.

trimmings into two oval shapes for the chest, reserving a pea-sized amount for later.

9 With one third of the remaining flesh, model two sausages for the arms measuring 2.5 cm (1 in) tapering each slightly. Bend near the bottom and pinch out elbows and stick in place. Make an oval-shaped head and ball nose using the remaining flesh modelling paste, flatten the face slightly and then indent the smile with the miniature circle cutter. Push the tip of a cocktail stick into the corners to create dimples.

10 Use one third of the remaining white modelling paste for the gloves. To make a glove, split this piece in half and roll a sausage shape, pinching gently at one end to round off for a hand. Press either side of the hand to lengthen into an oval shape and press onto the top to flatten slightly, without indenting. Make a cut no further than halfway down on one side for the thumb. Make three slightly shorter cuts along the top to separate fingers and smooth gently to lengthen, then press together and

bend round. To naturally shape the hand, push the thumb towards the palm from the wrist. Cut the end straight and stick in place on the arm with a tiny strip wrapped round hiding the join **(see below)**.

11 Thinly roll out red trimmings and cut out a miniature star for her chest and a small square for the belt buckle. Thinly roll out white and cut a strip for the belt and cut a

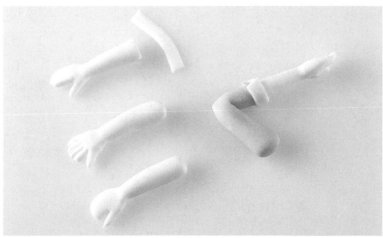

Modelling the gloves

Cupcake Undies

Imagine your guest's faces and the fun they will have choosing when you offer these fun cupcakes around. They're certain to liven up the conversation and make your party memorable!

YOU WILL NEED

- 12 x sponge cupcakes (see page 11)
- 1 tbsp jam
- Icing (confectioners') sugar in a sugar shaker
- Sugar glue and paintbrush
- Black food colouring paste

SUGARPASTE (see page 9)

- 100 g (3½ oz) white

MODELLING PASTE (see page 10)

- 10 g (¼ oz) mauve
- 15 g (½ oz) black
- 15 g (½ oz) red
- 10 g (¼ oz) dark cream
- 10 g (¼ oz) lilac

EQUIPMENT

- Pastry brush
- Small rolling pin
- 5 cm (2 in) circle cutter
- Plain-bladed kitchen knife
- A few cocktail sticks
- Blossom plunger cutter
- Miniature heart cutter
- Fine paintbrush
- No.1 plain piping tube

1 Brush the top of each cupcake with a little jam. Thinly roll out the white sugarpaste and cut circles to cover the top of each cake, smoothing around the outside edge of each to round off.

2 To make panties, thinly roll out mauve and black paste and cut the back and front shapes using the template (see page 77). To make bows, loop round tiny tapering sausage shapes of red and thinly roll out and cut long triangular ribbons cutting an angled end. For frilled edging, cut out a thin strip of white and press the end of a paintbrush over the surface gently pulling downwards to thin and frill **(see above right)**.

Cutting out panties

3 For the boxers, shape flattened squares with dark cream and black, making a small cut at the bottom to separate legs, pinching up a ridge on the bottom of each. Pinch along the top to open slightly. Using a knife, mark the fly and indent a line for each waistband. Decorate the black pair with red hearts cut from very thinly rolled out paste. To paint

the tiger stripe, dilute a little black food colouring with a few drops of water and paint uneven stripes over the surface. Use black paste to edge the waistband and fly, indenting little holes using the end of a paintbrush and filling with tiny red buttons.

4 To make the red heart thong, cut two thin strips of modelling paste and stick a small heart shape on the centre. For the red and leopard print male thongs, cut thin strips of black paste looping each round for waistbands. Model small oval shapes using dark cream and red, cutting the top of each straight so each sit neatly against the waistband. Paint uneven circles and dots for the leopard print.

5 The lilac bra is made by hollowing out a small ball of paste. Press gently in the centre, and then cut in half. Edge the top of each cup with a black frilled strip as before. Stick these cups onto a strip of paste and cut two thin straps. Indent the pattern using the tip of a cocktail stick. The black bra is made by modelling two ball shaped cups and use a small blossom flower to decorate the centre.

6 The red bra has flattened teardrop shaped cups, with indented pleats at the bottom using the end of a paintbrush. Use a blossom cutter to make the mauve flower shaped bra. To make the halter-neck bra, roll a small sausage of paste and then roll in the centre to make the neck strap, rounding off each cup. Press down to flatten and indent pleats as before **(see right)**. Stick in place on a long strip and mark the pattern using the tip of the piping tube.

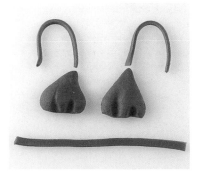

Modelling a bra

Birthday Treat

After a hard days work, give your man a special birthday treat with this fun depiction of a playful striptease.

YOU WILL NEED

- 25 cm (10 in) square sponge cake (see page 11)
- 30 cm (12 in) round cake board
- 550 g / 1 lb 3½ oz / 2 ¾ c buttercream (see page 8)
- Icing (confectioners') sugar in a sugar shaker
- Sugar glue and paintbrush
- 2 x sugar sticks (see page 10)
- Edible silver and gold powder

SUGARPASTE (see page 9)

- 400 g (14 oz) pale grey
- 1.25 kg (2 lb 12 oz) lilac

PASTILLAGE (see page 10)

- 115 g (4 oz) pale grey

MODELLING PASTE (see page 10)

- 200 g (7 oz) dark grey
- 110 g (3¾ oz) white
- 225 g (½ lb) flesh
- 5 g (just under ¼ oz) red
- 30 g (1 oz) black
- 5 g (just under ¼ oz) dark green

ROYAL ICING (see page 9)

- 15 g (½ oz) brown
- 30 g (1 oz) chestnut

EQUIPMENT

- Plain-bladed kitchen knife
- Serrated carving knife
- Large and small rolling pins
- Ruler
- Cake smoother
- 7 cm (2¾ in), 4cm (1¾ in), 3.5 cm (1½ in), 2.5 cm (1 in) and 5 mm (¼ in) circle cutters
- Palette knife
- A few cocktail sticks
- No.1 plain piping tube
- Small pieces of foam (for support)
- Medium and fine paintbrushes
- Scissors
- Small blossom plunger cutter
- 2 x plain paper piping bags

1 Slightly dampen the cake board with water. Roll out the grey sugarpaste using a sprinkling of icing sugar and cover the cake board, trimming excess from around the edge. Using a ruler, indent the radiating lines by marking down the centre first. Rub all over the surface with the silver powder and then set aside to dry.

> **TIP:** The long hair is helping to support the pose, but if you want to change the hairstyle to match the recipient, then use a large piece of foam sponge to support the figure until dry.

2 To allow for plenty of drying time make the pastillage table next. Roll out pastillage and cut a circle with the largest circle cutter. Indent radiating lines the same as the cake board surface. For the stand, roll a sausage with 5 g (just under ¼ oz) measuring 9 cm (3½ in) in length and set aside to dry making sure it is completely straight. For the supports, roll out the remaining pastillage and cut two circles of each measuring 4 cm (1¾ in), 3.5 cm (1½ in) and 2.5 cm

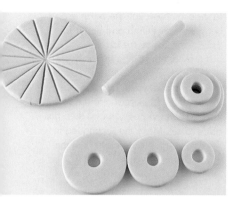

Assembling the table

5 To cover the back of the seat, first roll out 75 g (2½ oz) of lilac sugarpaste and cut two strips to cover either end and then roll out 770 g (1 lb 11 oz) and cut a strip to cover the back and front of the cake in one piece, reaching down to the top of the seat. Smooth gently along each edge either side to round off. With trimmings, cover the small area either side at the base and smooth the join closed with a little sugar glue. Using a ruler, indent even lines **(see below)**.

7 To make the man, first roll 135 g (4¾ oz) of dark grey modelling paste into a sausage 13 cm (5 in) in length for his trousers. Make a cut 2.5 cm (1 in) from the top to separate the legs and smooth along the edges. Pinch gently half way down for the knees and push in at the back to bend each leg. Stick in position on the cake leaving a little space at the base for the shoes. To make the shoes, split 10 g (¼ oz) of black modelling paste in half and shape into teardrop shapes, pressing down on each point to round off.

(1 in). Cut a small circle from the centre of each using the smallest circle cutter **(see above)**. Make sure that the stand fits correctly in each one. Stick the three circles together using a little sugar glue. Rub silver over the surface of all pieces and then set aside to dry, preferably overnight.

6 Roll out 175 g (6 oz) of lilac sugarpaste and cut a piece to fit the top of the seat, smoothing around the edge to soften. Roll out the remaining lilac and cut a strip to cover the front of the cake, softening the top edge and indent even lines as before.

8 For the shirt, roll 100 g (3½ oz) of white modelling paste into a teardrop shape and press down on the point to flatten for the neck area. Mark down the centre using the back of a knife. Indent buttons using the no.1 plain piping tube, and then indent little creases at each button and either side of the body using the tip of a knife so the shirt looks tight.

3 Trim the crust from the cake and level the top. For the back of the seat, cut a strip from one side of the cake measuring 15 cm (6 in). Trim out a slight curve from the centre, stand upright and then trim either side at the back so that the cake curves round slightly. Trim either side at the top to round off. For the seat, trim off each corner from the remaining strip and then trim a curve in the centre at the front and either side at the back, following the contours of the seat back.

4 Cut a layer in the seat cake only and sandwich back together with buttercream. Sandwich the two cakes together, spreading the underside of each with buttercream and assembling on the cake board. Spread a thin layer of buttercream over the surface of the cake as a crumb coat and to help the paste stick.

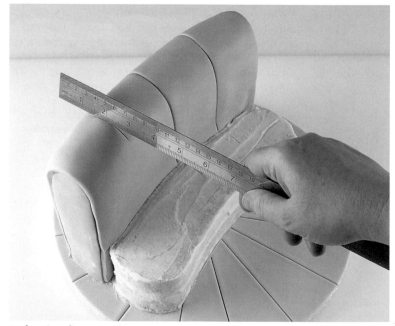

Indenting lines in the seat

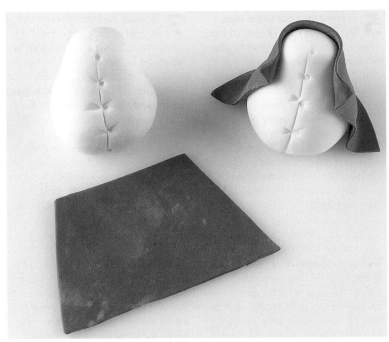

Wrapping the jacket around the shirt

9 To make the jacket, thinly roll out 35 g (1¼ oz) of dark grey modelling paste and cut out the jacket shape using the template (see page 77). Wrap around the back of the shirt and turn down the top two corners to make lapels **(see above)**. Stick the jacket and shirt in place on the cake, supported by the seat back.

10 Split 30 g (1 oz) of dark grey modelling paste in two and roll into the sausage shaped sleeves. Trim each cuff end straight and then bend each half way. For the cuffs, first split 5 g (just under ¼ oz) of white in half and set one half aside for later. Split the remaining half into two and roll ball shapes, indenting in the centre of each using the end of a paintbrush, making a hole for the hands to slot in. Thinly roll out dark grey trimmings and cut a strip for the collar measuring 6 cm (2½ in) in length. Cut out two square pockets.

11 To make the hands, split 5 g (just under ¼ oz) of flesh modelling paste in half. To make a hand, roll one piece into a teardrop shape and press down to flatten only slightly, without indenting. Make a cut half way down on one side for the thumb. Make three cuts along the top to separate fingers and twist gently to lengthen, press together and bend round. To naturally shape the hand, push the thumb towards the palm from the wrist. Pinch up excess gently at the wrist and stick in place inside the cuff. Make the opposite hand. Roll the white piece set aside earlier into a ball and press flat for the collar. Cut out a small 'v' from the front and then stick in place.

12 Make the legs for the woman next. Split 60 g (2 oz) of flesh modelling paste in half. Roll one half into a sausage. Bend one end round to make a foot, pinching gently to shape a heel. Roll the ankle area between your thumb and finger to indent and shape the leg. Push in half way at the back and gently pinch at the front to shape the knee. Stroke the shin to straighten, pushing out excess at the back to shape the calf muscle. Bend in position and then put aside to set. Make the second leg in the same way but straighten out the leg and point the toe.

13 For her body, shape 60 g (2 oz) into a fat sausage and then roll between your thumb and finger to indent the waist half way, rounding off the bottom. Roll the opposite end to lengthen the chest area and pinch up gently at the top to round off the neck. Press the front flat and then bend backwards to create an arch in the back. Stick in place on the man's lap using a foam piece to support in position. Stick the legs in place supported by a foam piece.

14 For her arms, split 25 g (just over ¾ oz) of flesh modelling paste in half. To make an arm, roll a piece into a sausage shape and pinch gently one end to round off for a hand. Press down on the hand to flatten only slightly, without indenting. Make a cut half way down on one side for the thumb. Make three cuts along the top to separate fingers and twist gently to lengthen, press together and bend round. To naturally shape the hand, push the thumb towards the palm from the wrist. Lay the arm down and push in half way, pinching out at the back to shape the elbow. Make a second arm and stick both in place supported by the seat. Push a sugar stick down through the neck area on both figures until only a little is protruding.

15 To make the man's head, first roll a 20 g (¾ oz) ball of flesh modelling paste and pinch out a nose. Open up the mouth area using the end of a paintbrush and mark nostrils underneath the nose. Push into each eye area to make a hole. Roll two small white eyes and for pupils, thinly roll out black paste and cut out two circles using the piping tube. Press each flat and then stick in place.

16 Just above each eye, stick on a tiny tapering sausage of paste for eyelids and then mark wrinkles in each corner using a cocktail stick. Stick on two tiny ball shapes for cheeks and blend in the join underneath using a little sugar glue **(see right)**. For ears, model two small oval shapes and indent in the centre of each using the end of a paintbrush. Stick in place either side of the head level with the nose.

Creating the facial expression

17 Put the brown royal icing into the piping bag and cut a small hole in the tip. Pipe the eyebrows. Cut a slightly larger hole and pipe the hair, spiking it up at the front a little. Leave to set, then using a little sugar glue, stick in place over the top of the sugar stick, pressing gently in place.

18 For the woman's head, shape 20 g (¾ oz) of flesh into a ball and pinch out a smaller nose than before. Stick on two tiny ball shaped cheeks, blending the join as before. For eyes, roll a tiny oval shape and cut in half lengthways. Stick in place with the straight edge at the bottom. For lips, shape a tiny piece of red into a sausage tapering at either end and press flat. Mark a line in the centre to separate the lips and push the tip of the knife into the top to indent the centre of the top lip. For eyelashes,

roll minute amounts of black into long thin tapering sausages and stick in place edging the bottom of each eye.

19 Using a little glue to secure, press the head gently in place over the sugar stick. The weight of the hair will need to be supported, so roll a 20 g (¾ oz) flesh sausage shape and stick in place wedged between the back of the head and the seat.

20 Split the remaining flesh in half and roll into the ball shaped boobs. Thinly roll out black modelling paste and cut out the woman's apron using the template (see page 77). Stick in place with a thinly cut strip for the waistband. For the bow, cut out four more small strips tapering two slightly at one end. Loop two round sticking ends together to make the bow and stick in place in the small of the girl's back.

21 With black trimmings, cut a black strip for the stocking tops and stick over the top of each leg. Cut out a tapering strip for the tie,

cutting a point into each end and stick in place draped over the woman's leg.

22 For the champagne bottle, roll the green modelling paste into a sausage and indent around the top. Thinly roll out white and black and cut labels, the black slightly smaller and stuck centrally onto the white. Stick a small, flattened ball of black onto the top of the bottle and a tiny flattened circle on the front. For the gold, moisten around the top of the bottle and a squiggle across the label with glue and leave until tacky. Sprinkle the tacky surface with gold powder, gently brushing away excess.

23 Put the chestnut coloured royal icing into a piping bag and cut a tiny hole in the tip. Pipe the very fine eyebrows. Cut a larger hole and then pipe the hair, building up little by little creating waves and covering the support. Pipe hair over the joins at shoulders. When the cake is dry, assemble the table securing with a little glue. Stick the champagne bottle in position on the table cloth.

Hot Devil

Here's a devilish stunner for your man to get hot and bothered about. Flaming with desire? He'd probably just burn his fingers!

YOU WILL NEED

- 20 cm (8 in) and 15 cm (6 in) round sponge cakes (see page 11)
- 35 cm (14 in) round cake board
- 550 g / 1 lb 3½ oz / 2¾ c buttercream (see page 8)
- Icing (confectioners') sugar in a sugar shaker
- Sugar glue and paintbrush
- 1 x sugar stick (see page 10)
- Red and egg yellow powdered food colouring
- A few drops of clear alcohol (e.g. vodka, gin)

SUGARPASTE (see page 9)

- 115 g (4 oz) red
- 400 g (14 oz) deep yellow
- 800 g (1 lb 12 oz) yellow
- 595 g (1 lb 5 oz) pale yellow

MODELLING PASTE (see page 10)

- 35 g (1¼ oz) red
- 5 g (just under ¼ oz) flesh
- 5 g (just under ¼ oz) black
- 200 g (7 oz) deep yellow

EQUIPMENT

- Plain-bladed kitchen knife
- Serrated carving knife
- Large and small rolling pins
- Ruler
- Cake smoother
- Palette knife
- A few cocktail sticks
- Small pieces of foam (for support)
- Medium and fine paintbrushes
- 2.5 cm (1 in) circle cutter

Rolling out the marbled cake board covering

1 Slightly dampen the cake board with water. Knead 115 g (4 oz) of red and 400 g (14 oz) of deep yellow sugarpaste together until marbled. Roll the paste into a long sausage to straighten the marbling then roll into a spiral. Roll out using a sprinkling of icing sugar and cover the cake board, trimming excess from around the edge **(see below left)**. Set aside to dry.

2 Trim the crust from each cake and level the tops. Cut a layer in each cake and sandwich back together with buttercream. Keep the cakes separate. Spread buttercream on the underside of the largest cake, place centrally
on the cake board and then spread a thin layer over the surface of both cakes as a crumb coat and to help the paste stick.

3 Roll out the yellow sugarpaste and cover the largest cake completely, smoothing around the shape and trimming excess from around the base. Smooth the surface with a cake smoother. Knead the yellow trimmings into the pale yellow sugarpaste and then cover the smaller cake on the work surface, trimming excess and smoothing as before. Spread a little buttercream on top of the larger cake and then carefully pick up the smaller cake and place centrally on top, smoothing again with a cake smoother to remove marks.

4 To make the girl, shape 25 g (just over ¾ oz) of the red modelling paste into a sausage and roll gently in the centre to indent the waist. Press down to flatten slightly, keeping the bottom at the back rounded. Cut the

top and bottom straight **(see below)**. Mark a line down the centre at the front using the back of a knife and then mark little holes for eyelets using a cocktail stick and criss-cross lacing with a knife.

TIP: To give the devil woman curly hair, simply twist each strand of black modelling paste into a spiral.

Components of the hot devil figure

5 Using one third of the flesh modelling paste, model the chest and neck area from a small sausage shape pinching up a neck in the centre. Stick in place on top of the body. Push the sugar stick down through the neck leaving a little protruding to help hold the head in place. Roll an oval-shaped head with a tiny ball nose using the remaining flesh modelling paste.

6 For arms, split 5 g (just under ¼ oz) of red modelling paste in half. To make an arm, roll into a sausage shape and pinch gently at one end to round off for a hand. Press either side of the hand to lengthen into an oval shape and press onto the top to flatten slightly, without indenting. Make a cut no further than halfway down on one side for the thumb. Make three slightly shorter cuts along the top to separate fingers and smooth gently to lengthen, then press together and bend round. To naturally shape the hand, push the thumb towards the palm from the wrist.

7 Lay the arm down and push in halfway, bend gently and then pinch out at the back to shape the elbow. Stick onto the body in an upright position with the hand turned outwards, supported with a piece of foam until dry. Make the second arm and stick in position with the hand resting on her hip. Roll out and cut a thin strip of red modelling paste to edge the join of each arm.

8 For hair, first wedge a small piece of black modelling paste behind the girl's head for extra support. The hair is built up with flattened teardrop shapes, larger ones first covering the main part of her head with smaller pieces over the top, swept over in one direction. Make tiny flattened teardrops

to edge around her face and two tiny oval-shaped eyes. Stick the girl in place on the top of the cake.

9 With the remaining red modelling paste model two oval shapes for her chest, a long sausage for the tail with a triangular shaped horn on the end and make two horns for her head. Support the tail with a foam piece until dry. Mix red powder with a little clear alcohol and paint her lips, indenting into the corners with a cocktail stick.

10 To make the flames, roll out the deep yellow modelling paste keeping it thicker along the bottom and cut into strips of around 20 cm (8 in). Using the circle cutter cut out semi-circles along the top, encouraging points where the circles overlap for flames **(see below)**. Stick in place as each is made, positioned around the base of both cakes. Cover the joins with smaller different sized flames.

11 When the cake is completely dry, dust the flames with red and yellow powdered food colouring keeping the red at the bottom and yellow over the top, brushing up to the top of the flames. Brush the excess sprinkles over the cake board and dust some red around the base of the girl.

TIP: When making the semi-circles for flames, twist each circle cutter slightly when pressing into the paste so you ensure you have neat, clean cuts.

Cutting out the flames

Templates

All templates are 82% actual size.

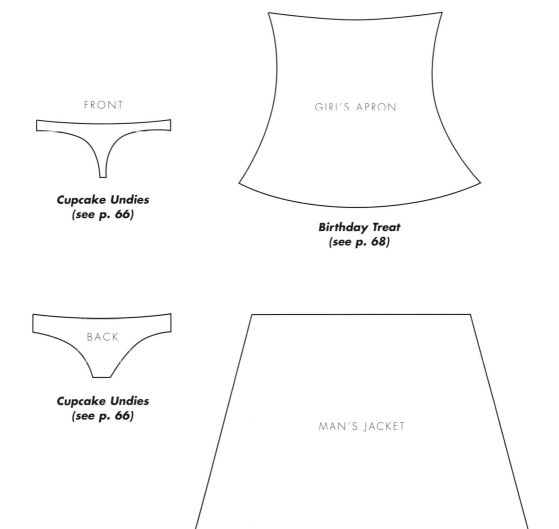

FRONT

Cupcake Undies
(see p. 66)

GIRL'S APRON

Birthday Treat
(see p. 68)

BACK

Cupcake Undies
(see p. 66)

MAN'S JACKET

Birthday Treat
(see p. 68)

Suppliers and Useful Addresses

UK

The British Sugarcraft Guild
Wellington House
Messeter Place
London SE9 5DP
Tel: 020 8859 6943

The Cake Makers Depot
57 The Tything
Worcester WR1 1JT
Tel: 01905 25468

Confectionery Supplies
29-31 Lower Cathedral Road
Cardiff CF1 6LU
Tel: 029 2037 2161
*Also outlets in Bristol, Hereford and
Swansea*

Culpitt Ltd
Jubilee Industrial Estate
Ashington NE63 8UB
Tel: 01670 814545
Website: www.culpitt.com
Freephone enquiry line:
0845 601 0574
*Distributor of cake decorations,
telephone for your nearest retail outlet*

Jane Asher Party Cakes
24 Cale Street
London SW3 3QU
Tel: 020 7584 6177
Fax: 020 7584 6179
Website: www.jane-asher.co.uk

London Sugarart Centre
12 Selkirk Road
London SW17 0ES
Tel: 020 8767 8558
Fax: 020 8767 9939

Orchard Products
51 Hallyburton Road
Hove
East Sussex BN3 7GP
Tel: 01273 419418
Fax: 01273 412512

Pipedreams
2 Bell Lane
Eton Wick
Berkshire
Tel: 01753 865682

Renshaw Scott Ltd
229 Crown Street
Liverpool L8 7RF
Tel: 0151 706 8200
Websites: www.renshawscott.co.uk
or www.supercook.co.uk

Squire's Kitchen
Squire's House
3 Waverley Lane
Farnham
Surrey GU9 8BB
Tel: 01252 711749
Fax: 01252 714714
Website: www.squires-group.co.uk
*Courses in cake decoration and
sugarcraft*
Online shop for specialist sugarcraft
products: www.squires-shop.com

Sugar Daddy's
No. 1 Fisher's Yard
Market Square
St. Neot's
Cambridgeshire PE19 2AF

NEW ZEALAND

Chocolate Boutique
3/27 Mokoia Road
Birkenhead
Auckland
Tel: (09) 419 2450

Decor Cakes Ltd
Victoria Arcade
435 Great South Road
Otahuhu
Auckland
Tel: (09) 276 6676

**Golden Bridge Marketing
Wholesale Ltd**
8 Te Kea Place
Albany
Auckland
Tel: (09) 415 8777
Website: www.goldenbridge.co.nz

**Innovations Specialty
Cookware & Gifts**
52 Mokoia Road
Birkenhead
Auckland
Tel: (09) 480 8885

Milly's Kitchen Shop
273 Ponsonby Road
Ponsonby
Auckland
Tel: (09) 376 1550
www.millyskitchen.co.nz

Spotlight
(branches throughout New Zealand)
Wairau Park, 19 Link Drive
Glenfield
Auckland
Tel: (09) 444 0220
Website: www.spotlightonline.co.nz

SOUTH AFRICA

The Baking Tin
52 Belvedere Road
Claremont
7700
Cape Town
Tel: (021) 671 6434

Confectionery Extravaganza
Shop 48, Flora Centre
Ontdekkers Road
Florida, West Rand
1724
Johannesburg
Tel: (011) 672 4766

South Bakels
235 Main Road
Martindale
2092
Johannesburg
Tel: (011) 673 2100

Party's, Crafts and Cake Decor
Shop 4, East Rand Mall
Rietfontein Road
Boksburg
1459
Johannesburg
Tel: (011) 823 1988

Chocolate Den
Shop 35, Glendower Shopping Centre
99 Linksfield Road
Glendower
Edenvale
1609
Johannesburg
Tel: (011) 453 8160

Jem Cutters
128 Crompton Street
Pinetown
3610
Durban
Tel: (031) 701 1431
Fax: (031) 701 0559

South Bakels
19 Henry van Rooijen Street
Bloemfontein
9301
Tel: (051) 432 8446

AUSTRALIA

Cake Art Supplies
Kiora Mall
Shop 26 Kiora Rd
MIRANDA
NSW 2228
Tel: (02) 9540 3483

Cakedeco
7 Port Phillip Arcade
228 Flinders Street
Melbourne
Tel: (03) 9654 5335

Hollywood Cake Decorations
52 Beach St
KOGARAH
NSW 2217
Tel: (02) 9587 1533

Susie Q
Shop 4/372
Keilor Rd
NIDDRIE
VIC 3042
Tel:(03) 9379 2275

Cake and Icing Centre
651 Samford Rd
MITCHELTON
QLD 4053
Tel: (07) 3355 3443

Petersen's Cake Decorations
370 Cnr South St and Stockdale Rd
OCONNOR
WA 6163
Tel: (08) 9337 9636

Gum Nut Cake and Craft Supplies
SORELL
TAS 7172
Tel: (03) 6265 1463

THE NETHERLANDS

Planet Cake
Zuidplein 117
3083 CN Rotterdam
Tel: (010) 290 91 30
Email: info@cake.nl

SOUTH AMERICA

Boloarte
Rua Enes De Souza
35 - Tijuca
Rio de Janeiro
RJ - CEP 20521-210
Brazil

NORTH AMERICA

Calijava International School of Cake Decorating and Sugarcraft
19519 Business Center Drive
Northridge
CA 91324
Tel: (818) 718 2707
Website: www.cakevisions.com

Maid of Scandinavia
3244 Raleigh Avenue
Minneapolis
MN 55416

Wilton Enterprises Inc.
2240 West 75th Street
Woodridge
IL 60517

Home Cake Artistry Inc.
1002 North Central
Suite 511
Richardson
TX 75080

Creative Tools Ltd.
3 Tannery Court
Richmond Hill
Ontario L4C 7V5
Canada

Index

The Author and Publisher would like to thank Renshaw Scott Ltd for supplying the Regalice sugarpaste used throughout the book.

For details of other titles and information on sugarcraft tuition, see www.debbiebrownscakes.co.uk